Remember the Nails

ISBN 978-0-9979021-1-2

Cover art by John Hoke

Edited and formatted by Shannon Janeczek, PublishSavvy

All scripture taken from the NEW AMERICAN STANDARD BIBLE®, © Copyright 1960, 1962, 1963, 1968, 1971, 1972, 1973, 1975, 1977, 1995 by The Lockman Foundation.

The "NASB", "NAS", and "New American Standard Bible" are Trademarks of The Lockman Foundation.

Used by permission.

Remember the Nails:

40 days of Doing Something Uncomfortable on Purpose

Steve Schofield

Remember the Nails:

40 days of Doing Something Uncomfortable on Purpose

Steve Schofield

Many thanks to my wife, Cindy, and my three sons, Marcus, Zach, and Tayler, for supporting me—and putting up with me.

To Doug and Debra Hinken for listening to the story that one Sunday afternoon, and for helping spark the direction of this project.

To all the willing churches, the Greenville 1073rd National Guard, the City of Greenville and Danish Festival officials, and several individuals who helped make the Clean-up Greenville successful. It was awesome to ask God's people, who responded, and helped make the event a success.

Thanks to Scott Forsyth, Kim Cain, Pastor Bart Hall, Sunday Quinn, and Pastor Joel Heron for sharing your uncomfortable stories.

And thanks to our Lord and Savior Jesus Christ, for doing the most uncomfortable thing anyone has or will ever do, dying on the cross!

Contents

Wood

Nails

Spear

Result

How I Was Inspired to Write the Book

The journey started in February 2012. God had plans for me to write a second book before I was done with my first, *52 Pickup: These are the words I give to you to share with everyone.* He was laying the groundwork for material that would inspire me for this book. I didn't even realize it at the time, being so focused on the *52 Pickup* manuscript. I was also involved in a student ministry, teaching middle school boys.

The student ministry received a gift that allowed us to send the entire youth staff to a teaching conference. The headline speaker was Kyle Idleman, who, as of the writing of this book, is the Teaching Pastor at Southeast Christian Church in Louisville, Kentucky. Kyle's church is one of the largest churches in America, and he is the author of *Not-a-Fan: Becoming a Completely Committed Follower of Jesus*.

The book's focus is on the fact that you are either a FAN or FOLLOWER of Jesus. While attending the conference, they provided everyone with a free copy of his book. I didn't immediately read the book, but planned to eventually.
What I took away from the conference was this: I was confident in my walk with Jesus. I was more a follower than a fan. So I didn't think too much more about it.

Fast forward to the summer of 2012, where I just finished my three-year commitment teaching middle school boys on Sunday mornings. I wasn't sure what my next ministry involvement would be. I knew God had something in store; I just wasn't sure what it was. I was planning to have a relaxing summer, doing some fishing with my youngest son Tayler. The only other plans were to finish editing the *52 Pickup* manuscript, and being a technical editor on a technology book.

Of course, God had other plans for me. In June of 2012, I started reading *Not-A-Fan*. After completing the first chapter, I didn't want to continue reading the book. The material challenged my walk with the Lord. I thought I was doing pretty well until I'd read it; suddenly I had doubts. I was left thinking, "I'm not doing as well as I thought." I struggled to read the next chapter, but the material really spoke to me. It was the most challenging book I've read to date.

I've read various books on my journey that also spoke to me and made an impact, but not quite like *Not-A-Fan*; it really rattled my soul to the core. After most chapters, there was a short section from a guest author. The guest author would then summarize how God impacted their lives and how they became a follower of Jesus. They were very impactful and emotional stories.

After about a month of reading the book, I had four chapters left. I decided to just finish and be done with it, no matter the outcome. It kind of scared me, honestly; I didn't know if my outcome might be as dramatic as quitting my job, and wait for God to point me in the next direction. After finishing the book, one of the few times in my life, I was confused what I was supposed to do. I felt a strong conviction to do God's work. The main items I took away were:

- I wanted to consider myself a follower of Jesus
- I needed to do something that would put me out of my "comfort zone… on purpose"

About a week after finishing the book, the morning of Thursday, July 5, 2012, I turned out of my driveway to go to work and there was trash blown into the street. There had been a storm during the night. I initially drove past the trash, trying to ignore it. By the time I was about two or three blocks away, the small still voice in my head said, "You should go back and pickup that trash." I remember thinking that I wanted to get to work early. But if I didn't turn around and go pick up the items, I would regret it all day. The thought I had was: "Steve, it will only take about 10 minutes to pick up the trash and you'll still make it to work early." I turned my car around and went back. As I parked along the street, two trucks that passed by me. I felt a little awkward and didn't really want people to see what I was doing. But from what I could tell, I was alone and no one witnessed me picking up the trash.

As I was driving to work, an idea came to mind about a project. It went something like this: "You should coordinate an event to pick up trash in your hometown before the local annual festival." The festival is held the third weekend in August. Since this was a few weeks away, I did not mention the idea to anyone for a couple days. After waiting two days, I asked my wife if she'd help, and she agreed. My logic was that if she agreed, then I should move forward.

I started to think about how I was going to pick up all the streets in my hometown. I couldn't do this project alone. That evening, I finished working on a friend's computer, and they needed it right away, so I took it back to their house. While driving there, I saw a police car sitting and watching traffic. I stopped and asked the police officer, "How many streets are in my hometown?" He wasn't sure, but suggested I could talk to the City Engineer. Then I remembered the City Engineer lived just a few blocks away. I was excited to share the idea with him.

I stopped by his house the following Sunday. I was pretty sure he would know the individuals who coordinated the local festival. He put me in contact with everyone I needed. While I was talking to him, his wife was smiling. She stated, "Tell Steve what has been bugging you the last couple of days." Apparently on Saturday and Sunday, he was running on a local trail and noticed some trash, so he stopped and picked up trash, both days. This left him feeling a little annoyed. The same day, I stopped by in the afternoon to propose the idea for the clean-up. Some would call it coincidence.

His wife mentioned that she liked the idea and would talk to her small group; they probably would be open to "adopting" an area to clean up. This is where I got the idea to involve other churches and organizations to "adopt" an area.

I used the information the engineer provided to contact others who coordinated the local festival, and other city officials. They provided me a list of areas that needed to be cleaned up. This information helped me formalize a plan.

The next step was to work out a priority list of what needed to be cleaned up. I didn't have a clear plan of when it would happen, and I planned on visiting churches near the various spots to propose that they clean up an area close to their church, or in their neighborhood. My initial strategy was to perform the clean up during the second weekend in August, approximately one week before the festival. I visited a couple of locations and they were open to the idea.

When I was working with my church, it was a little unclear if they would accept, because one of the proposed clean-up days was Sunday. At the time, we were going through a sermon series on the Ten Commandments. Of course, one of the things about honoring the Sabbath is not to work. I figured that since I work in computers, picking up trash wasn't something I do on a regular basis, so to me the clean-up wasn't work.

When I floated the idea around, there was some resistance. Looking back, asking people to perform work on Sunday was probably not the best idea. I thought most people would be available on Sunday, and I was motivated to make sure the project was completed according to the schedule. I didn't want people to be interrupted too much in their daily lives and Sunday is one weekend day they could help out. The idea of spreading the clean-up over a two-week period, however, *was* acceptable. Instead of trying to do the cleanup on one particular day, they had the flexibility to work around their schedules. This approach was a huge success! This was a great idea God provided and probably the most significant reason people helped out. I honestly didn't care when an area was done, as long as it was done during the two-week timeframe; all I needed to know was the time that they would perform the work. I needed this information to turn into the city and the festival coordinators. My goal mostly was to make sure no one called the police on our clean-up crews.

I started visiting more local churches and organizations. Each time, I would stop by unannounced. I approached people and asked for their commitment, discussed what area they would clean up, and I mentioned I would follow up with them to get this information. To my surprise, everyone stepped up to help with this project. God opened doors, and many local churches and other organizations adopted portions of the city. Around 30 locations were targeted to be cleaned up. The city even contracted trash bins to be delivered a couple of weeks earlier, so people could drop the trash off at the local community center.

Looking back, it strikes me how everyone was so open to the idea. I expected not too many people would be open to an idea from a complete stranger. All I knew was that my goal was to bring the various denominations and other organizations together to make things happen in God's name. The good Lord REALLY motivated me to do this.

It was interesting to hear stories about the project later. Some people made it a time of fellowship, and prayed for their neighborhood. Others had contests about which group could pick up the most trash. There were dead animals, clothes, and one item every almost person mentioned was the amount of cigarette butts they picked up. I believe this was their "doing something uncomfortable… on purpose."

While cleaning up a particular location, I met the police officer who I originally asked how many streets were in Greenville. He was nice and thanked us for cleaning up our town. The main theme of the entire project was to "Clean-Up Greenville" and "do something out of your comfort zone... on purpose." This was the part of the new book's title, but I hadn't realized that yet.

On the last day, the clean-up project was almost complete. I got the sense we needed to end on a good note. While cleaning up the last location, a person, who happened to be named Sunday, found a necklace that was in the shape of a fish, with the word Jesus on it. I knew right then, the project was finished.

When the project was all done, all locations were clean, and there had been more than enough help. Not only was the clean-up project a huge success, the local festival had awesome weather and turnout. Praise God!

Uncomfortable Testimony by Sunday Quinn

My name is Sunday. I have attended church on and off all of my life. I found a church in 2010 that I began to attend regularly, but after the death of my father in 2011, and the end of an 11-1/2 year relationship, I stopped going to church. My life began to unravel and I didn't even realize it. I found myself in financial dire straits, lost, pulled away from my children, family, and friends. My priorities were all messed up, and my life was on a fast track to nowhere. I felt guilty when I did pray, only because I had stopped... unless I was in a situation. I felt I was using God only when it would benefit me.

In late July of 2012, I started feeling a pull to get close with God again, to get my act together, because I realized I was slowly losing everything I had. Through a whirlwind of events that did not make sense until later when I found my way to GCC (Greenville Community Church), and was placed in the paths of some amazing people. I started attending regularly, going to small groups, getting involved.

This time when I was going to church, I found myself with a want: to learn, to pray, to grow. As a result, I found my life starting to turn around and change. I used to worry all of the time about everything: where rent would come from, how I was going to put food on the table, get gas for the car, interviews, and my kids; life in general. Now I have handed my worries to Jesus, which was not an easy, comfortable thing to do. However, the more I do, and see the results, the easier and more comfortable it is for me.

I have only worked for 2-1/2 months of the last 15, yet I have shelter for my children, food on our table, and all of our basic needs taken care of. I have learned while we may not have all that we want, through the Grace of God we have all that we need.

- Sunday Quinn

What's in a Name?

Later in the summer of 2012, after the Clean-Up Greenville project was complete, our church was doing a sermon series on *Becoming a Contagious Christian,* by Bill Hybels and Mark Mittelberg. One of the sermons covered different styles of sharing the Word.
For those who know me personally, my natural style is to be direct; some would say "blunt." I would agree with both assessments.
The pastor asked me to talk about how I used my style in the Clean-Up Greenville project, which was more direct, or "in your face."

When I was in the recruitment phase of the project, I would literally make a cold call to a location, searching out the head pastor, or person who was the decision maker. I would go un-announced and asked them if they had a few moments. I would introduce myself, why I was doing the project and give a summary of the story. I don't like cold-calling salesmen or telemarketers contacting me, so the interesting thing was that I was doing exactly that when recruiting others in the project. I was literally obsessed with finding churches or anyone who would or could help out.
It was amazing watching God work through me, and allow so many to be part of something special.

I had the pleasure of visiting Israel in the spring of 2012, a few weeks after attending the conference at which Kyle Idleman spoke. My favorite location we visited was the Garden of Gethsemane in Jerusalem. I felt the presence of the Lord and it "just felt like home." I can't explain it, but after visiting the Garden and praying the Church of All Nations, I felt my journey to the Holy Land was complete.

While visiting the Garden, I saw plaque that mentioned Luke 22:42 (NASB) 42. It says, "Father, if You are willing, remove this cup from Me; yet not My will, but Yours be done." I figured if Jesus could go through what he went through, I could handle being uncom-fortable asking God's people to give a couple hours to pick up trash. Between reflecting on the feelings I had while asking people to help, and visiting the Garden, the saying "Remember the Nails" came to me.

When I gave my testimony at church about my style of approaching people, I borrowed a 9-inch (22.86 CM) nail and held on to it while I was talking.   People mentioned later that my point was very clear, and the nail helped with that understanding.   Unlike my first book, where I literally wrote all the stories and God revealed the title later, this time around I had this really cool title first: "*Remember the Nails : 40 days of doing something uncomfortable...on purpose*." I wasn't sure what the theme of the book was, I just knew the title.

A few months went by; the *52 Pickup* manuscript was complete and was off to the printer. The good Lord revealed to me one day, "You remember that awesome title I gave you? It'll be a 40-day devotional asking people to do something for the kingdom. It can be prayer or something else, but the idea is to get out of their comfort zone for 40 days." When I was talking to our Compassion Director at my church, she added one additional question: **"What on Earth are you doing, for Heaven's sake?"** I thought that was a pretty neat saying and thought I would include it after every poem in the new book.

As you begin your journey, remember a couple of things:

- "What on Earth are you doing, for Heaven's sake?"
- Remember what Jesus did for us. When you find yourself uncomfortable doing something in His name, remember Luke 22:42.

What's in a Layout?

Towards the end of putting together the layout of *Remember the Nails* manuscript, I had the forty poems organized into four sections, with ten poems in each section. At first, I planned on having the theme of American football. Section one would be called first and 40, section two was second and 30, section three was third and 20, and last was fourth and 10.

To my pleasant surprise, I discovered that the layout God revealed has a biblical meaning and communicates a message that goes along with the book theme. The title includes forty days. Jesus spent forty days in the wilderness fasting and being tested (Matthew 4:2). When Noah was on the Ark, it rained for forty days and forty nights. (Genesis 7:12). Paul was flogged five times 40 times minus one in (2 Corinthians 11:24). My pastor mentioned it was believed if a person was flogged 40 times, they would die, so a person was flogged 40 times minus one (39). This goes along with the first three sections of the book poem count.

The poems are still categorized into four sections, but the first three contain thirteen, which was the number of people at the Last Supper (Matthew 26:20-25). The last section only contains one story, and you may wonder, "Why just one?"

I decided to switch themes. The first section is now called *Wood*, because the cross was made of wood. The second section is called *Nails*, which Jesus had pounded into his hands and feet. The last section is called *Spear,* which was used to verify he was dead. The last section is called *Result*, which contains one poem called *Wounds*. When Jesus returned, he showed Thomas (John 20: 24-29) His wounds. We only have one Savior, which is the result; there is only way to the Father (John 14:6).

As the title states, *Remember the Nails*. Each time you do something that is not Christ-like, you are contributing to the pain

Jesus felt while hanging on the cross. He bore sins for all people, for all time, while on the cross. That is a chilling statement.   I'm thankful Christ Jesus did that for me and all of mankind.

I wanted to share the lengths the good Lord goes to when prompting me to write my devotional books and the meaning behind them. They have subtle, yet powerful meaning.   As you read, remember the layout has special meaning as well.

Target Audience for the Book

Is this book for you? From the very beginning of this book project, the word *uncomfortable* has been mentioned time and time again. When I was prompted to clean up trash, asking people I didn't know for help, and asking the local newspaper to do an article about the project, each of these things was something I'd rather not do. I prefer to stay in the background, where it's safer and more comfortable.

Remembering what Jesus did for us is something we can't even come close to matching. All we can do is be obedient, and try our best to be his hands and feet. The book *Not-A-Fan* convinced me to get out of my comfort zone and made me reflect on my journey. I realized I wasn't where I thought I was in my walk with Jesus.

The goal of this book is for me to be obedient to God's prompt to share my story, and hopefully the forty poems will inspire you to take your own journey. I read somewhere that when we reach the end of our comfort zone, we begin at God's, getting closer to Him. Stepping outside your comfort zone is worth the risk, and the rewards are awesome.

Ask yourself each day when you first wake up, "What *Kingdom work* will I try to attempt today?" It can be as simple as prayer, leading a small group, starting a ministry, picking up trash, or something else. God will lead you, we just need to listen and follow. I recommend the first thing you do is pray and wait; God will lead you and the decisions will become obvious. It might not be easy or comfortable, but doing the right thing isn't usually either.

God bless,

Steve Schofield

SECTION 1 —Wood

This is the first step of your journey; you might not have an idea of how things will go. Getting started is usually the hardest step, especially when things could start to be different and make you feel uncomfortable. Humans are conditioned not to seek uncomfortable things. Even from an early age, we are taught to stay away from danger. Facing our fears, however—including a fear of heights, speaking in front of people, failure or rejection—is an important part of maturity.

When leaders—no matter what their field—are the first in their circle to do something, their friends, family and others will often doubt that the adventure will be successful. They say things like, "You are going to fail," "That's just crazy," or they reject the idea all together. Only after many attempts, usually failing multiple times, does someone learn from their mistakes and start to succeed. Only then does the circle of supporters rally to their side.

When you are doing the Lord's work, especially when trying new things, you always have the Creator on your side. He has plans for you, as mentioned in Jeremiah 29:11 (NASB): "For I know the plans that I have for you,' declares the Lord, 'plans for welfare and not for calamity to give you a future and a hope.'"

Interesting that the Lord mentions plans and hope, and not calamity. When starting on a new journey, knowing that you are likely to be uncomfortable, the word *hope* is a comforting thought. As you progress in these first thirteen days, remember hope. The Lord is with you. Pray for guidance as you move forward. Don't be afraid to fail, because you will learn as you go along in your adventure.

Uncomfortable Testimony by Pastor Bart Hall

One situation that makes me uncomfortable is when I step into the unknown. In life, this makes me over-prepare for new places or experiences. When it comes to following God, it can be quite an experience. A mentor many years ago told me that, as a pastor, I needed to have God release me from ministry before I left any churches. But, this also meant that I would be ready to resign before I knew where my next ministry placement would be. What would this mean for my family? How would I take care of my wife and the kids God has blessed me with? This unknown was a major stressor both times that it happened.

But when I really think about it, as a pastor, my job is to help people follow God's lead. If this means I should resign before I knew what my next job would be, then so be it. Even though it was un-comfortable, I would rather be uncomfortable following the lead of God than be comfortable not following the lead of God. The first is a recipe for being fulfilled, while the latter is a recipe for being more uncomfortable and less fulfilled in life. Even though I know this, it is still hard to follow God as the Leader. It came to a point that I just had to make the decision, because I knew if I did not, I would not be pleasing God.

In hindsight, I see how God had the whole plan in mind all along. Once I had made the decision the first time to leave a place of ministry, I was hired within two weeks at the second place. The second time, I did not get a job as quick, but I knew that I would have one in God's timing. Now, it makes it a lot easier to follow God's lead whenever I feel he calls. It helps in church decisions, family decisions, and everyday life.

- Bart Hall

Day 1 – Absence

Scripture

Acts 3:1-10, 4:1-21

Poem

Not being present, not being around
Not being available, not being found

Everyone knows when something is absent
They might describe it differently

They know something is not quite right
They tread through life

Even though they are absent of something
Void of something, we can't put our finger on it

There are many types of absences
Temporary, Permanent, Not complete, Not finished

Some are physical, some are emotional
All leave the same type of absent feeling

When we realize something is missing
We long for the one thing; we desire to return to where we were

We think the feeling of loneliness will disappear
Our lives will return to normal

We live with a false hope
Stumbling around every day seeking to be satisfied

The media tells us we "need" one more thing
We need that thing to be satisfied

This false absence is created

If you don't have this or that

You are not quite complete
You are not quite whole

Our society is in an unknown state
What people believe is subjective

There is no plain truth, no plain justice
When something bad happens, there are moments of silence

There are flags put at half-mast
Honoring those who have fallen, showing respect for the absence
in our life

This is all well and good
For those left behind

Unfortunately, only in times of absence and tragedy
People ask for prayers, comfort and guidance

It's a novelty to acknowledge God
Only when bad things happen

I just don't get it
I can't explain my frustration

This side of heaven creates an angst
When others don't agree, an absence of agreement

Peter and John performed miracles for many to see
Many believed in the result

Yet others still wanted to doubt
But they couldn't doubt in the outcome

Although they didn't want to believe
They couldn't deny; people were able to see what changed

Our society is at a crossroads

God is absent in a majority of people's lives

Although they see changes in people
They continue on with their ways of the past

Man cannot fill this absence
Man cannot fill this void

Only the Holy Ghost can complete someone
When they accept Jesus as their Savior

Men will continue to stumble
Denying the absence exists

In the end, we all will be together for a short time
Some will last, some will not

All we can do is hope
People don't ignore the absence in your soul

Because before long, that temporary absence on earth
Will become permanent, separated from the one who loves you
most.

Amen!

Story Behind the Poem

As I watch various tragedies unfold in the media, we see people
hurting, people mourning. My heart goes out to them, yet the
media doesn't quite acknowledge our Creator. The media appears
to look only for what feeds and creates a negative tone. Maybe
this is just my perception, but I get frustrated with it.

The days of minding our own business, not gossiping and having an
opinion about everything is gone. Social media provides this false
closeness, yet it lacks the one basic thing: face-to-face interaction.
People can't discern the emotion from the person typing their
sentences online. We have multiple generations who can't seem to
communicate face-to-face. A message here, a text there, all sent

without emotion. The words state the message, but the human element is not with it. Even as I type the description behind this, I can't quite put my finger on it. It's an incomplete description of my frustration: I feel like I can't change it, or make a difference.

God uses these stories to help describe what is happening at a moment in time. Atheists, liberals, and others attack conservatives and basic morality. It hits home, and I'm sad for them.

The other part of this story covers another subject: death. It is a permanent separation from those who love you on Earth.
My uncle was suddenly killed and it impacted our family. He was a larger-than-life character who was so funny. When he entered a room, peoples' reactions were always the same: they smiled and looked forward to talking and listening to my uncle.   I think every family has that one person who makes everyone laugh, and everything they say is "just funny." It doesn't matter what culture you are from, there are people who make those around them smile, and he was one of those people.

I was reading the book of Acts, when I came across the story about Peter and John healing a beggar (Acts 3:1-10). Even after people witnessed it, the authorities wanted to know who gave power to Peter and John, when they plainly stated Jesus Christ, the one who they crucified, they STILL did not want to believe. The next part of the story is covered in Acts 4:1-21.

The religious authorities at the time showed ignorance to the plain truth, which seems similar to what is happening in society today. Although many people can see the results, they still deny the reason for them.   They keep on denying the absence of God. All believers can do is pray and give this over to God, because he is the one in control.

Day 2—Alone

Scripture

Matthew 25:23

Portions taken from Matthew 25:23 (NASB)
"...Well done good and faithful servant..."

Poem

Absent, Void, Bare
Feelings of loss

Single, Peaceful, God Fearing
Feelings of refreshment

Time away, Time to reflect
Thinking about what really matters

Reflect about the past
Review the present

Contemplate the future
Planning for the best

We are not alone when born
We are not alone when death comes

We alone face judgment from our maker
Hoping for the magic words

We are only one step away from meeting Jesus
Make sure while on Earth, you pray a lot, pray often, and pray hard

Ask Jesus for guidance
About every task, every question, every problem

He can help provide guidance

So you do not end up alone

With Jesus in your life
You are NEVER alone

When driving to work
When going on a trip

We are designed to be social
The world glorifies going at it alone

You are on the Earth maybe four score
You are in eternity forever

Man can't imagine forever
They can imagine four score and seven

Jesus, thank you for coming to Earth
So we are not alone in eternity

Amen!

Story Behind the Poem

One day I was reading articles on how connected the world has become. It amazes me how small the world has become using the Internet, social media, texting, email, and face-to-face technologies. All these things allow for people to communicate to one or many (including millions) of people. The one thing it doesn't provide is in-person communication.

There is nothing like being in a room of people trying to communicate ideas. I've played a part in projects that literally took months to discuss a single idea, and come to a consensus on all points. Regardless of whether the topic is simple or complex, trying to communicate ideas without personal interaction is much more difficult. Technology offers flexibility, and allows people to reply to topics on their 'own time.'

While technology will continue to evolve and impact people's lives, one of the side effects of doing things on our own time, is that we get lonely. When accepting Jesus as your Savior, a person is not alone. They have the Holy Spirit to help with guidance on any topic. Although we are connected more than ever, I see articles that show people are 'discontent' more than ever.

This story helps categorize and reflect on how humans are meant to interact, and not handle things alone. When humans attempt to do things alone, in the long run, they'll be lonely, even though they could be classified as a success. I'll take an eternal relationship with the creator any day, over the temporary one mankind offers.

✝

Day 3—Attacked

Scripture

James 1:26, Matthew 11:30

Poem

You ever felt like every time you turn around,
There is something seemingly in your way?

No matter how much you prepare.
No matter how much you plan.

Something always seems to get in the way.
Every obstacle appears to get larger and more difficult.

It's like someone is having fun watching you stumble.
Roadblocks are put up everywhere.

You work through one really hard roadblock.
Another pothole comes along out of nowhere.

Finally, things appear to have calmed down.
A much larger pothole suddenly appears.

After a few battles that appear to impact the overall plan
Anxiety, worry and uncertainty rule the day

It seems the harder you work
The harder the task at hand becomes

Nothing is easy, although the task is rewarding
It requires a lot of mental heavy lifting

Up until this point, you have kept it contained
The journey has been great

When you widen the effort to include others,

The battles become larger and more difficult

You've entered the arena of many thousands now
The goal is no longer contained

The idea becomes shared with others
Attacks are more widespread, impacting many others

Who is engaged in the battle?
The enemy has drawn the battle lines

The effort is to restore souls
The efforts are to repair hearts and turn them back north

North to God, his son Jesus and Holy Spirit
The enemy has made it clear: every soul will be a battle

Nothing will be easy, nothing will be calm
There will be bumps, potholes and obstacles along the way

Not a moment's rest
Not a moment's peace

Scripture tells us to endure the journey
Take refuge in the Son, for his yoke is light

There will be peaks and valleys
Endure the everyday with hope provided from above

Keep it simple; take care of orphans, widows at the least of these
An orphan can be a child; it can be a middle-aged person's struggle
with addiction

Even an older person, lost in their way
Each orphan has their own unique story

God wants all of his "children" to know he loves them
He wants to see them come to him with their hearts open

God will restore hope from their pain

God will help overcome their bad habits

And even when we have hang-ups from time to time
He'll be there, loving us unconditionally

For the Good Book says
One day you will be with him in his house, forever

What a comforting feeling knowing we are loved
By such a great Creator

This single hope helps us endure
The journey filled with hurts, hiccups and hang-ups

Amen!

Story Behind the Poem

One Sunday at my church, a video was played that introduced a new ministry called People Restore. It was presented by a man who explained that the ministry was to help people restore their faith back to Jesus. There were *hiccups, hurts and hang-ups*. Every person who walks with Jesus has these, and to varying degrees, they can interfere in his or her life.

The mission was to take back others who have been distracted. I was moved and seemed to connect with the key people in the ministry. I mentioned the stories God has blessed me with and it seemed to be a place I can share with others. I'm not certain of the outcome or how involved I will be personally, but it seems like a next step, and I wanted to be part of it.

We were at a Bible study around the same time we saw the video, the same person who introduced the ministry asked for prayer, mentioning they were under attack since announcing the ministry. I don't recall the exact methods they were being attacked, although when trying to do the right thing, the obstacles become more frequent.

God laid on my heart the word "attacked," and the first sentence/phrase used in this story. We also had just studied the scripture in our small group. As with other stories, I receive various prompts, and there were enough of them to write Attacked.

†

Day 4—Bad Taste

Scripture

Proverbs 24:13, 27:7

Poem

Something has soured to the point of tasting bad
Some candies are made to be sour

These candies make your mouth water
There is a slight twinge of sweetness, although the sour taste
almost overwhelms it

You try this food, after a while it sours
You try that food, after a while it sours too

I'm not sure what causes the sour taste
There is a certain odor and the bad taste gets burned into your
long-term memory

There are situations in life you try for a while
Which are like food

At first, the situation tastes sweet and satisfies;
After a while, there is a slight difference in your experience

The experience creates a seed of doubt
It makes you ponder and reflect

This could be the enemy fostering these feelings
You start to see situations that used to be there, although they are
slightly different

You try hard not to remember the bad experience
You pray, asking for forgiveness and a glass half–full attitude

Other situations appear ever so slightly

Making you wonder if your instinct is trying to tell you something

You ignore your instincts, hoping the situation will recover
I'm not certain of the outcome, but I remember Jesus is there
through it all

The situation can reveal itself as a bad mental taste
Making a person really wonder

Like anything, if something sours, pray for forgiveness
Pray for the situation to resolve itself.

If something bothers you mentally, use the word of God as a guide
Follow the instruction to correct through honest dialog
It's God's right to pass judgment alone

People will let you down, food will let you down
God won't let you down, although at times it might seem that way
When going through something,
The taste might not be quite right...

Keep tinkering, trying, and praying
God will not let you have a bad taste of his love; it will be sweet
and enduring!

Amen!

Story Behind the Poem

It seemed for a while, regardless of work or personal situations,
most everything I was involved in would start off on the right track,
and then would sour. I would try something else for a while, and
then that would sour. Through God's love, I was able to work
through it all, and find where God wanted me to be.

Doesn't that always seem to happen? You find yourself in a great
situation; you go along with the crowd, and then - bam! Life moves
on for some, changes for another. Before long, your situation has
changed; the chemistry isn't the same. Things begin to sour and
change occurs. Being able to adjust with changes and adapt is

something God has us on, and it's a journey—an ever-changing journey!

†

Day 5—Big God

Scripture

Psalm 8:3

Poem

You are a big God
Bigger than anything or anyone

No one can fathom
Your size or your thoughts

You are sovereign
You created us with free will

God, in a few months
8000+ will ascend in your name

They will be seeking something
Many are not sure of what

Some will come down from the North
Others from the South, East and West

Their minds will be like clay
They need something to influence them

They will need someone to shape their thoughts
Some will realize you sooner than others

Some will be guided by your helpers and teachers
Please inspire your helpers to guide these young minds

The helpers, guides and teachers alike
Seek your truth, guidance and wisdom

These 8000+ can influence the next generation

We ask and pray your bigness to show

We ask for your bigness to guide, and eventually lead
Others to your son Jesus Christ

This will be a huge event, not as big as you
We all know, you are a big God

If you want to do big things in everyone's life
Go Big, and eventually, Go Home to your Big House!

Amen!

Story Behind the Poem

Several youth staff from my church and I attended training in
Louisville, Kentucky. During a break from one of the sessions, the
staff had a prayer time in the arena that was going to host the
following year's conference, which would be attended by
highschoolers. One of the leaders was describing the various
planned activities, and where they will be hosted in the convention
center.

The building is 140,000 square feet. The building is big, the effort
to get the conference up and going is big, and the goals are really
big! While walking around, the Holy Spirit prompted me to sit
down and write this story. What struck me was the size of the
building and the amount of participants attending; they were
planning for more than 8,000 people.

I was able to share this story with a person who was going to be
involved with the conference. The person mentioned they were
inspired and expressed the large effort it was going to take for the
conference to be successful. Our meeting was brief, but I had a
sense the conference would be awesome.

The intentions were pure, they wanted to glorify God and bring the
story of Jesus to thousands who would attend and influence the
next generation. A Big event to glorify our Big God!

One related item to this event, the book *Not-a-Fan*, written by the speaker, Kyle Idleman, was the inspiration for *Remember the Nails*. It never fails to amaze me how our Big God works.

✝

Day 6—Blunt

Scripture

Matthew 26:52, 16:1-12

Poem

Stating what is on your mind without thinking
That is the first way of being blunt

Not being polite to another
That is the second way of being blunt

Being emotional and lashing out
That is the third way

I'm sure there are other ways of being blunt
No matter how you look at it

No matter how honest you want to be
When stating something without love or compassion

The look on a person's face, will be something to see
When you first meet a person, a first impression is made

If your intention is to be honest
Make sure you think before you speak

A bad first impression lasts a while
It takes even longer to overcome

Take it from someone who knows
It is not easy to undo

I've spent a lifetime
Making bad first impressions and trying to recover

People will always be a bit guarded

They will wonder what will be said next

There was something recent
I have no idea where it came from

Something was said, not meant to be bad
After some thought, it made me feel sad

An apology is good place to start
Hope your relationship can handle it

Our Father in heaven
Can use anything, anyplace, anytime for good

He can even take something bluntly said
And turn it into something glad

It can become a story
To share with others

Peter spoke without thinking sometimes
Like the time he drew his sword
As Jesus stated in Matthew 26:52 (NASB)

"Then Jesus said to him, 'Put your sword back into its place;
For all those who take up the sword shall perish by the sword.'"

Jesus was being straightforward
As this was the time to fulfill his destiny

Being straightforward and honest
But try to use tact, this will get you farther

Jesus' words were straightforward
It offended many in his day

Because when they questioned him directly,
He didn't give in and say what they wanted to hear

"It's a fine line being honest and compassionate

Some do it better than others"

Our Lord and Savior did it the best
Sometimes His words seem sharp

After prayer, reflection and thought
The Holy Spirit will help you understand

There will always be a next time
Try to do it better, don't go at it alone

Ask our Father in heaven for guidance
His advice will help provide a positive tone.

Amen!

Story Behind the Poem

Over the course of my life, I've said things I regretted. In my younger years, I was known for speaking my mind and most of the time, it was pretty raw. I didn't give my words a second thought and my intention was to shock others around me. Spending a lifetime of undoing bad first impressions is difficult. I'm glad the Lord allows people to be compassionate, patient and kind— especially teachers and coaches!

What sparked this story was something I had said to a good friend. It came out of nowhere, and wasn't meant to be bad. After some thought, it reminded me of my youth, and of being bluntly honest. I knew better. My friend's initial reaction was to be surprised and I almost immediately apologized. He didn't seem to hold it against me, though. Maybe this was God's way of using that situation for another story.

The next time you offend someone, be the bigger person and apologize. Don't say you're sorry just to make yourself feel better, either, but to genuinely show compassion and let them know it didn't come out right. Ask for forgiveness. Sometimes it won't happen right away, but try to learn from your mistake, and not repeat it.

Day 7—Borrow

Scripture

Proverbs 22:7

Poem

How much does it cost to break up a relationship?
Ever borrow something you never returned?

Could be money, tools or something else...
Do you feel guilty?

Why do you feel guilty?
Do you avoid contact with the person you owe something to?

Even though you liked the person
You don't speak or have contact

Ever break something that isn't yours?
What feelings do you get?

Do you return it broken?
Or do you replace the item?

In all cases, something negative happened
Someone trusted you to borrow an item

Regardless if it was money
Or something else

You were trusted by someone else
To use their resources on your behalf.

Understand one thing, when you borrow
You are borrowing from your future

If you don't have enough now and you borrow

You will need more in the future, more than you have now

People assume they will have more in the future
Bigger, Better, More of More

At what point when you borrow
Can you not pay back what you owe?

How long will you be in denial?
When do you determine you will take steps?

The Good Book mentions
The borrower is at the mercy of the lender

Sacrifice is needed to get back to the beginning
Doing without is a necessity

Instead of giving into wants constantly
You have to do without, and get out of debt

Some grasp at straws to win the Lottery
They think their problems will be solved

All you do is trade one set of problems for another
It might take a while to realize

Mankind doesn't like being told the right way
They think they know best

When they get to a point -- once they've figured out
Their way isn't the best way -- they aren't sure what to do

Pride sets in, divisions happen
Compromise isn't an option because they don't know how

It took the sacrifice of Jesus on the cross
To pay for our debts

For all time, for all people, for all eternity
He did it out of love

He even went one step further
He delivered the truth

All he expects in return is our heart
Our obedience to his word

Thank you Jesus for showing how to sacrifice
For showing how to deny oneself to better the cause

Even though we are stubborn
Jesus is patient, kind and waiting at the door, to forgive our debts.

Amen!

Story Behind the Poem

There were a few things that were involved in the writing of the
story. The first example: A person once owed money to me and
was given a specific date to repay it. They didn't show up or call.
We tried to contact them a few times and hadn't heard back.
The relationship has been broken for now. I'm sure in the end
things will be OK; it could take years, and all over just a few dollars.

Secondly, I borrowed something from a loved one and never
replaced it. They haven't asked for it yet, but I still need to
replace it!

Around the time I was writing this story, the U.S. government
was struggling, with no end in sight, for a compromise between
legislators. Our President was telling Congress they needed to
act before "falling off the cliff." This statement was used to
describe our government and how they would not have the
ability to borrow money to pay its bills. It's frustrating and I have
to be careful to not let it bother me.   The worrying over the
situation doesn't do any good, and the media only covers the bad
news anyway.

Lastly, in the theme of the 40 days of doing something
uncomfortable on purpose, the idea of borrowing something and

never repaying the debt, or returning an item, can cause strained relationships, which is uncomfortable. If you have a situation like this, repay your debt or work something out. Don't let an insignificant amount of money or a material object ruin a relationship. A clear conscience is a good thing to have!

†

Day 8—Drift

Scripture

Hebrews 2

Poem

Accepting God is a rush
In the beginning, you feel invincible

You seek him, he reveals himself
The more you seek, the more you find

The more you find, the more pieces you discover
It's like a never-ending maze

Things come along, causing you to drift
One moment, you are walking with God

Neck deep into God's journey
The next minute you are distracted

Things drift ever so slightly
You used to pray daily for all sort of things

The world offers a rush
With the right amount of money

You can feel invincible
No one can touch you

Instant gratification feels great
Seems like nothing can go wrong

It can happen while on vacation
It can happen when you least expect it

The passion once felt for God
Can drift like a piece of wood in a river?

Old habits return, anxiety returns

It only takes a couple of reminders

To drift back towards God …
God's word is like a paddle

It can keep you on the journey down the river
It can be used to hit upside the head

To stay on course with God
Requires regular checkups

This helps prevent drift
In your walk with Jesus

Denying God is something he doesn't like
It's a risk not worth taking

It's ok to take breaks from everyday life
Just remember to not drift from God

Amen!

Story Behind the Poem

I had an anxiety attack several years back, and it's something that is on my mind frequently. It's one of those things that always seems to be a cloud overhead, that could burst into a storm at any moment. I believe it's a blessing that the Lord gave me, to remind me of my life before accepting Christ.

When I took a recent extended vacation, I didn't keep up my regular devotionals, prayer, and confession, acknowledging his power, and thanking him for all good things. It only takes a few days of drifting from a regular routine to have temptation, like anxious feelings, return. This is something I don't enjoy. I always thank God for his patience and for letting me drift, and reminding us that He is still here.

Day 9—Edge

Scripture

Matthew 11:28-30

Poem

You arrive at a familiar place one day
The mood is tense

You try to be cordial
Other people are not so

They are heads-down working
Don't have time to talk

When they talk to you
It is as if you are being talked at

You have their best interest at heart
Although your pride wants to say otherwise

You try to understand better
They seem to not pay attention

I won't take the time to figure it out
All I believe is it's not something I did

They are saying it is your problem
Your problem alone to figure out

At that moment, pride kicks in
It puts you on edge

Anger sets in, the shields go up
You are dead set on proving them wrong

You know for certain the problem is theirs
But you don't know how to compromise

You talk to others to get their input

They are cordial and help talk it through

Although you know what is right
The pride wants you to hold tight

When they don't want to accept the situation
They want to believe they are right

Being on edge opens the door for the enemy
Being on edge spiritually puts you towards a cliff

Falling off will only prove one thing
The fall won't kill you, the landing will

Make sure when you are on the edge
And the gravel starts to give

Take a moment, do yourself a favor
Hand this angst over to Jesus

Let him deal with it
He'll hold his hand out to help you away from the edge

Even if you fall off
If Jesus is with you holding your hand

The outcome will be different...
Jesus's wings are big enough to support you both

He'll provide the landing you need
Even if the landing is a bit firm, it will be just right

It might take time
To realize the landing Jesus provided was what you needed

Be patient, be kind and forgiving, and engage all sides
This will take the edge off and in the end

All sides will appreciate the softer approach

Amen!

Story Behind the Poem

I observed a situation in my personal life where multiple people, including me, were working very hard and were on short deadlines to complete a project. There was an issue; I don't recall the details or the project. What upset me was that I wanted to focus on one thing to resolve the problem, and others were not paying attention to my suggestions; they were ignoring me. Their actions and attitude put me on edge. I took the situation personally and began to get confrontational. Although I knew better, my emotions impacted my better judgment.   I was being blamed for some of the problem, even though I couldn't fix it, the lack of control upset me.

I've been through this type of situation before so I know the solution: it is not for me to judge and go at the fight alone. Handing these things over to Jesus is the only way (for me at least) to resolve what seems to be an unresolvable problem. I can't count the times I've been working on something and completely forget to stop, just for a moment to pray for guidance... when I do it, amazingly the solution happens.   I call it "invoking the Divine intervention rule," also known as praying.

Day 10—Everyday Porn (*Porneia* in the Greek)

Scripture

1 Timothy 6:9-11

Poem

Modesty has taken a back seat
People show more and more

What is displayed for everyone to see?
Is expected to be shared by some

In the world today, Porneia is available almost everywhere
It's in books, on billboards, commercials and online

The appearance is subtle, though, not revealing everything at once
A little here, a little there of the forbidden

Porneia generates an interest for its observers
But they are really victims; they just don't know it yet

Sensations are increased temporarily
The long-term effects are devastating

Porneia is relentless, we are wired to react
When we see something that looks nice

Men are wired visually by design
It only takes a glance, a brief look to be engaged
The brief high seems so innocent

The images we see stay much longer
This can wire the brain differently than God intended

The definition of beauty starts to change and become confusing
We start comparing to what we have

Everything starts to get bland
We get bored with normal and seek other avenues

Porneia is appealing, yet so addictive
Even a glance is too damaging to risk

No one knows what the standard of beauty is supposed to be
Porneia's intention is to lure someone into its grip

Get them addicted to something they can't have
Change their heart and turn away from everything else

It kills its victim in a different way
Desensitizing to most everything

The enemy twists God's perfect design
Many are impacted by its effects

Physically, emotionally and spiritually
All senses are enhanced from the love we feel for our spouse

God intended our spouse to be our definition of beauty,
nothing else
The world today has twisted this particular fact so much

The words in Songs of Solomon are God's design
The world has taken this design and altered it beyond recognition

Extraordinary measures have to be taken
To overcome the effects of the alterations

Nothing man made can overcome it, we are not strong enough
God, we need your power to help overcome the misuse of your
perfect creation

For only He has the Grace and Mercy to overcome anything
To undo its effects, one needs God's power

Amen!

Story Behind the Poem

This story was written after reading a book by Mark and Grace Driscoll, called *Real Marriage: The Trust About Sex, Friendship and Life Together.*

It seems as the old saying goes, "sex sells." If you look at commercials, billboards or most any advertising, a good portion of what you see will have a subtle sex appeal to capture your attention. Personally, it's something I have to resist. The idea of modesty has been altered by the last couple of generations. Unlike other parts of the world, the West seems to glorify people being skinny, not a healthy weight. Some models are so skinny; it gives young ladies the wrong impression. On TV, a good portion of the commercials cover products and gadgets related to weight loss.

There is nothing better than watching your diet, exercising regularly, and getting good rest. This is the only tried-and-true way to maintain a healthy body, at least for me. Regardless of if you agree with the Driscoll's book or not, it is an issue we all have to face.

One additional note about why I used the word *porniea* instead of porn or pornography. My Pastor covered this word and its meaning in a sermon around the time I wrote the poem. Here is a link that covers more information on this translated word: http://www.biblestudytools.com/lexicons/greek/nas/porneia.html

Day 11—First

Scripture

John 20:24-29

Poem

Scheduled for a specific time
Show up right on the dime

No other person is around
For the time being, I just sit down

Waiting for someone, anyone to come
I send messages out

Asking if I was wrong
No answers about

I wait, wait and wait some more
This is an odd feeling

Being first to something
Being ahead of the curve

Then I realize, I'm normally the last one there
Late for everything most times

People expect you to be late
Or right on time, which is my norm

The odd feeling of being first
Not sure of everything

Cutting the path, arranging things for others
Many in the world don't like being first

After many moments, answers come back

You are not wrong, we are coming

So sit back and relax
We are coming; you are just ahead of the curve

Later in the day
I realize being first in something

Usually causes most people to be uncomfortable
They are unsure, cautious and feel alone

Being the first at something
Usually attracts doubts and even some critics

Why are you doing that?
No one else is doing that!

The first person to doubt Jesus was alive
Was his disciple Thomas - and look at what happened

This is where the description "doubting Thomas" came from
This saying is used even today
(I wonder if Thomas realized he would be famous?)

For one little doubt, Jesus responded so tactfully though:
(John 20:29) Jesus said to him, (NASB) "Because you have seen
Me, have you believed? Blessed are they who did not see, and
yet believed."

The next time you doubt

Or are the first at something
Realize He was the first and you are not alone

He is with you
Every step of the way

It might not seem that way to you
Sit back and ponder, and know you probably are not "the first"

Even if you are, your Savior is right there
Walking the walk with you

I believe in Jesus!

Amen!

Story Behind the Poem

This was based on a day when I was invited to lunch with some friends and I showed up on time for the event. No one else was around. I'm normally the person who squeaks right in - barely on time - to most things. I don't like being too early. It was an odd feeling sitting there alone, unsure if I went to the wrong location. After about ten minutes, I got a response from my friends; they were coming. It was a relief!

The story of "the First" didn't hit me until later in the day. My wife and I were headed to an event for my son, when I realized the scripture I read earlier in the day about Doubting Thomas was related. I laughed, and realized I probably needed to write about it.

Being the first person to an event, or the first to perform a task or figuring out something new, causes people most times to be uncomfortable. It still amazes me when things like this come together. I hope when you are the first at something, remember that you probably aren't, but it sure feels that way! The more you walk with Jesus, the more times you'll be doing things that feel like the first time. Rest assured, I didn't think I would be writing Christian devotional books. I would have been called "Doubting Steve" if Jesus talked to me face to face.

Day 12—God Sense IS the Sixth Sense

Scripture

Proverbs 3: 5-6, Hebrews 11:1

Poem

When you can see something
When you can touch something

When you can feel, taste or hear something
We know it's real; we have earthly evidence

God gave us five senses to use
Sight, Smell, Hearing, Taste, Touch

There is a sixth sense not talked about much
It's God's sense... we can't categorize it like the other senses

A majority of people in the world today
Don't want to humble themselves to acquire this sixth sense

It takes God talking through little children
To show us God's world is simple

We have theologians, professors and other smart people
Trying to explain God's word

If we worked as hard trying to obey His words
As we did trying to explain or avoid them

Our world would be a different place, I'm sure of that.
The closer I grow to Jesus

The more my heart hurts. I can't physically force
Or mentally persuade a single individual into accepting Jesus

It's only a choice a person can make themselves

It has to be between them and God

A three- or four-year-old can plainly state "Jesus loves you"
Without pretense, without judgment, without wanting something
in return

This is pure, real love. Only when we plug into the sixth sense
Do we start to discover what life is meant to be

Man doesn't have all the answers
When we try to explain and claim we have the answers,
pride sets in

Which is plainly wrong, and not something God approves of
Here's the crux: Loving Jesus is simple, and we make it hard

For man, following His ways is not easy
We are such selfish creatures

When we are little, we are unselfish, we are real.
As we age, we become less real and jaded by the world.

No one is old in heaven, everyone is young
I've not seen this for myself, but a little pure one says so

I have faith that Jesus exists, and God exists
But I don't have all the answers

Some may say I'm crazy
Believing something that isn't "real"

When you plug into the God sense
You see things differently

For now, we have a choice to make
Chose our own path, or God's

From others' witness and my own experience
I have chosen God's path

There are many unknowns to come
We do know the final outcome: God wins, the enemy doesn't
This doesn't stop the enemy though

Guard your heart, your pure God-loving heart
It's worth it in the end

When things get tough, seek God's wisdom
He is listening, waiting for his children to plug in

Amen!

Story Behind the Poem

This story was inspired by the book *Heaven is for Real.* I've read *90 minutes in Heaven, 23 minutes in Hell* and this book. These are the three books I usually recommend to non-believers.

I struggle with non-believers, or those resistant to accepting Jesus as their Savior. There were many examples in each of these books that convinced me. Between my own experience writing stories, and reading these experiences, I know God is real. I can't explain it, but I know.

I struggle in the world today because we have so many distractions and devices that were supposed to make life simple. The way this little boy described the simplicity of Heaven only confirm my beliefs. I have three boys, and can relate to how they describe things so clearly.

At times, I wish my poems were as simple, but God is using me for a different purpose. I'll keep sharing!

Day 13—Grace and Mercy

Scripture

2 Corinthians 12

Poem

How fitting are these two gifts
Some people have a hard time accepting

Some can't let go of baggage
All you have to do is lay down your worries

For his yoke is light
Some feel they have to carry a burden

An entire lifetime to feel worthy
All this feeling does is weigh you down

And fills your soul full of worry
No one can earn Grace and Mercy from God

He alone can give this gift
If he so chooses

Some would say that is harsh
People have to realize he is a JUST and Sovereign God

All he wants is our heart
All he wants is us to give 100% of us to him

The scriptures state God's grace abounds
Men cannot fathom its reach

The first two commandments are the most important
Love your God with all your heart, mind and soul
Love your neighbor is the second commandment

That is a tough one
For some people are harder to love than others

These are the ones Jesus states we should follow
We should pray an extra prayer

For one day you could be surprised
This person could come to you and thank you for sharing Jesus

Don't make it complicated
To accept God's Grace and Mercy in your life

The enemy will try to harden your heart
And make it so you are comfortable in that, so you will drift away

God is God, we are not
The more I learn about God

The more I do not know
The more man tries to make his message complicated

Through theology and various descriptions
When you read God's Word, the words are clear

Grace and Mercy for all who accept his love
Through Jesus Christ our Lord

Amen!

Story Behind the Poem

Grace and Mercy were two words that came to me one day. The world and its many forms of media don't encourage Grace and Mercy towards one another. God speaks to Paul in 2 Corinthians 12:9: "My Grace is sufficient."

When we have discomfort, we become very focused on our own problem. I'm not a very good sick person. I'll admit that. I'm impatient and just want to feel better. Those who are closest to me notice it the most. I don't show much grace or patience. It's a good thing I don't get sick very often.

Despite our own problems, we need to continue thinking of others first before ourselves. The Bible mentions we are to take care of orphans, widows and the least of these. It amazes me anytime we go serve others, we forget about our own problems and challenges. We realize our problems aren't as big as others. Those who are less fortunate are truly grateful while we do our best to show grace and mercy towards them.

For those who have more patience and compassion than I, may God bless you and help strengthen those who are like me and don't have these gifts. God showed his grace when he sent his son Jesus Christ to die on the cross, that is the ultimate example of Grace and Mercy.

✝

SECTION 2 – NAILS

Congratulations, you have made it the first thirteen days. Have you taken an inventory of how you are doing? Does it seem a little easier thinking about doing Kingdom work every day? Or are you still getting the swing of it? Are you feeling a little uncomfortable?

God calls us to be disciples and use our gifts to further the Kingdom. You are 33% complete in your journey to a new beginning, doing Kingdom work every day. God is guiding you and providing direction every step of the way.

Do you have a quiet time? Do you set aside a certain time of the day where you spend time in prayer, talking to the Creator? Sometimes slowing down is the right medicine; this can help provide clarity and direction on things happening in your life. I challenge you over the next 13 days to write down your thoughts and prayers. Keep track of what you pray for and write down the outcome. God will answer prayer in certain ways you might not expect.

You might say, "Steve, I don't have time to do this." Take literally 5 minutes, wake up that much earlier, or go to bed 5 minutes later. I'm sure you can spare that in your daily life. Ask for God to guide you and see what happens; you might be surprised.

Turning over issues to God is one way to help free your mind and soul to focus on Kingdom work. It's exciting, yet causes us to be a little hesitant in the beginning; because we aren't sure it's safe. The message of the next 13 stories is to continue on the journey, doing God's work every day. The effort can be small or large, but no matter the size, if it impacts others, it's worth it.

Uncomfortable Testimony by Kim Cain

Over the years, I've come to realize my comfort zone is getting so big, it's almost non-existent. Things have changed quite a bit since I first started walking with Christ, though. Every day is an adventure.

In my early walk with Jesus, I was not comfortable around people. I was very shy, and I recall thinking all I needed was my animals, Jesus, and my family, and life would be just fine. I was walking with Christ and he had some serious plans for me, I just didn't know it yet.

An opportunity came up at my church to become the compassion director. This entailed overseeing ministries related to providing compassion to the church and the community, such as blood drives and our food pantry. It meant working with people who were in need, in all kinds of areas. Some of the challenges included working with local or state agencies to help those who come for assistance. I trusted God for everything, and He provides for all of the ministry's needs.

With God leading my ministries, miracles happen daily! I thank God and praise him for everything he does. With God, all things are possible! I will continue to lean on him for everything I do.

Continued blessings!

- Kim Cain

Day 14—Gridlock

Scripture

John 15:25

Poem

Frustration, anger, sense of helplessness
Pride, positioning, no compromise

Humility is not displayed by anyone
If either side is not willing to give

This can happen on the road too
Too many cars trying to fit

During certain times of the day
Congestion, stop, go, stop, go

There are situations where you are just caught in it
Things were moving along smoothly

All of sudden, you are sitting there
Not being able to control your own destiny

Gridlock is not healthy for anyone
Each battle is a mini-war

Blood pressure goes up, defenses increase
Each driver thinks they are right

What is right? Whose side do we take?
When two individuals who differ on something
Neither can control their thoughts or actions of the other party

Since each person has free will
This can create gridlock between individuals

How you react, is up to you.
The Good Book has all kinds of stories about our Savior

He was put in situations where others didn't agree with him
One time he let out his frustration

He cleared his father's house because it turned into a marketplace
Not a place of worship; He wanted it to remain Holy

How Jesus reacted is a good lesson to all
He did nothing for himself, but for everyone else

The next time gridlock or a disagreement occurs
Step back and evaluate the situation

If you fall to pride and try to take a strong position
The other side most likely will do the same

Nothing will be accomplished
Just hard feelings, it will cause strain

No one wins and hard feelings remain
Until we recognize we are not in control

One greater than us, is
The world today does not like to compromise

You are told you can have it your way
And that when the end comes, gridlock will not occur

You will face the Creator
With every spoken word, every thought you had

You have a choice and free will
A gift from the Creator

Because he loves you
You might not understand it fully, but you have it

The next time gridlock occurs, recognize it

When you have a relationship with Jesus, you are not alone

Hand tough things over to him
You will make it through, with him in control

He will help you navigate, through the gridlock of life
In the end, standing alongside you

Amen!

Story Behind the Poem

Many stories I read and comments disagree our country was founded on Biblical values, including the Ten Commandments. This is the crux of the issue: many want peace and joy, which occur when living by the Bible, but also many want it their own way and resist living by the Word. There is an increasing pressure on society to remove God and anything Christian.

The gridlock of traffic and politics in Washington, D.C., is a glimpse into the world we live in today. No one wants to neither give up anything nor be humble enough to see things from the other side. Everyone can see things aren't right, but they are using their own values to determine what is right, and won't give in. People like to claim they are humble and know what is right.

On this side of heaven, when gridlock occurs, it's frustrating. Then when something bad happens, and both sides see it, each side blames the other when both are affected. All along, they knew the problem that was about to happen could impact both sides.

When someone thinks they remain in control, gridlock happens in their soul. This can only be freed up when we turn control over to God. In my opinion, much of the gridlock is caused by not having a Biblical standard, which is to think of others and not themselves. They deny Jesus and his examples.

As Jesus states in the Bible, John 15:25 (NASB) "But *they have done this* to fulfill the word that is written in their Law, 'They hated Me without a cause.'" People want it their own way, but are not willing to accept bible-based Christian values; they seem to resist without knowing why.

✝

Day 15—Heart

Scripture

Psalm 17:3, 26:2, 139:23, Romans 14:13-23

Poem

The heart is selfish
The heart is deceitful

The heart gets jealous
The heart is spiteful

The heart takes things wrong
The heart is prideful

The heart holds onto things
The heart wants more

It keeps score and won't let go
Even if I try

Holding on so tight
Distracts us away from Christ

These distractions can cause others to stumble
Jesus states "do not cause others to stumble"

When the enemy sees the distractions
He swoops into increase them

The distractions cannot be easily undone
We need to seek God's heart

God's heart is generous
God's heart is kind

God's heart is so big

No one can fathom

When things come up
That seems so big

All we have to do is give him our hearts
God's heart can handle all things

God, I desire for my heart to be pure
God, I desire for my heart to be all yours

No matter what has happened
I want to hand it all to you

I pray for all my brothers and sisters
I pray for them to seek Christ first

It does not matter how they seek you
As long as they do, that is all that matters

This is my prayer to you
I seek your heart and to be more like your son

He provided the perfect example
No matter what people did to him

He was forgiving, patient and loved them
So the struggle continues

A part of my heart wants to continue down its own path
This leads to destruction

I pray for forgiveness, ask for repentance
God... I ask you to forgive my heart

I ask you to come examine my heart, oh Lord
Help my heart seek your path, not its own.

Amen!

Story Behind the Poem

It was the summer of 2012; I was coordinating a project to clean up parts of my hometown. I was passionate to get this project up and going and I was working hard to get volunteers to participate.

It's my nature that when I'm facing some kind of struggle, I wake up in the middle of the night, thinking of the best ways to complete the task. Obviously, this causes me to lose sleep.

After a few days of not having a lot of sleep, I became impatient and my heart hardened a bit. When visiting potential volunteers, I expected them to jump on board right away, since this was a God-inspired project. When that didn't always happen, I got frustrated.

I wrote this story to help overcome the anxiety and express some of the negative feelings I had one day. When I finished reading the poem, it reminded me of scripture King David used in Psalms about the heart. As King David mentioned in, Psalm 26:2 (NASB) "Examine me, O Lord, and try me; Test my mind and my heart." I felt the enemy was using my gifts (the coordination and drive to do God's work) against me. As the scripture states, guard your heart.

Day 16—In between

Scripture

Matthew 4:4, 2 Timothy 3:16-17, Hebrews 4:12

Poem

In life, we start going forward
Then something goes bump in our journey

We start going backwards
We stumble for a while

Then we recover and start moving forward again
In the middle of it all

We can go both backwards and forwards
We think progress is being made

We are really in between, going nowhere
Our world is in between things all the time

I'm not sure we really go forward
As much as we think

When we seek God's vision
We tend to feel more comfortable and things seem right

When we seek our own vision
We tend to think we are going forward

When we are really going backwards.
Life is a choice.

You can try to go forward on your own
Make a go of it

Or you can wait, yes, wait a minute

Pray and seek guidance.

When we wait, we are not going forward
But when we wait, we are not going backwards either.

You are in between things while waiting
This feels awkward because

Some feel they need to be doing something all the time

Busy, busy, busy
People like to be busy; then they think they are going forward

The next time you catch yourself saying
"I don't have enough time"

I challenge you to go against the flow
I challenge you to wait and see the outcome

When this challenge arises,
Seek God's wisdom with a quick prayer like this:

"God, I'm feeling really rushed here
Not making headway

I seek your guidance, wisdom and knowledge
I know you will assist me."

When you are done, take a deep breath
Look to the sky and check your perspective

The brief wait will help you stop going backwards
And start going forward... With God's direction.

Amen!

Story Behind the Poem

My personality is such that I need to feel busy all the time. For the last several years, God has blessed me with having side projects that keep me busy. It could be a variety of things: a side job running a content website, writing a book, or being involved in my kids' life. Whatever it was, the side project was something usually time-intensive.

It's hard for me personally to just sit around and not do anything. If I push too long, I actually start going backwards, even though I think I'm moving forward. As the poem states, keeping busy tricks people who don't like boredom.

One of the things I've learned in my walk with Jesus is that we all need downtime. We need a change of pace from the everyday busy-ness. My challenge from this story, if you catch yourself overloaded, is find a friend to watch the kids, have your spouse perform some chores, and take a weekend to get away from everything. No TV, no radio, no Internet. At first, this will seem odd, and you might feel "off," but when you return to your regular life, you'll appreciate the downtime and see a difference.

Day 17—Infected

Scripture

Acts 2:1-13

Poem

Ever had a paper cut?
How did it feel?

It was uncomfortable, yet not too bad
But every time you bump the area

You are reminded of the pain
If left unattended, redness can set in

If not treated, it can become infected
The once-little paper cut can be something more

A little prevention in the beginning
Could help you avoid additional pain

Life is like a paper cut with
Various levels of pain

In the beginning, the pain is almost nothing
It takes a bump to remind you something is not right

As the pain grows, the annoyance requires attention
It could get bad enough to require medical intervention

Limbs can be lost, life can be changed forever
And it all started with a tiny cut

Sin is like a paper cut
It's something our souls have when we are born

As we grow older, our exposure to sin grows

Like a small cut, your soul becomes infected and more painful

You try to self-medicate
Drugs and alcohol are common, of various kinds and amounts

These can be taken daily, when we're trying to hide and forget
the pain
As we stumble through life, God never leaves us

He waits for us to look to him for the medical attention for our soul
He is the ultimate healer

Only he can take sin away so we are healed
When we seek his medical advice (the Bible)

He provides the right amount of medicine at the right time
Before long, the little cut that turned into something bad

Is healed, and he is using you for his Kingdom
Sharing your story of once being infected

Now you are healed and lean on him
The world is sick and infected

Although it can seem like a paper cut
It doesn't take much to need serious attention

Only God can provide the necessary medicine to prevent
From being infected by the world.

Amen!

Story Behind the Poem

I hadn't exercised in a few weeks because of some pain in my lower
back. Due to my lack of exercise, my anxiety returned for a few
days. Exercising, in addition to being a healthy choice, also helps
keep my anxiety away. My lower back issues had been happening
for a few months, and I was ignoring them. After a few visits to the

chiropractor and one visit to a deep tissue massage therapist, my back felt fine. But when I attempted one day after that to exercise, my lower back issue returned.

My wife and I went shopping one day for various things. She mentioned that I should get some new shoes to see if it would help with the lower back issue. I have been wearing a particular type of brand of shoe for over 15 years. I tried a different brand, and although they were comfortable, they seemed to be causing the issue with my lower back to be worse. The fact is that I usually have lower back issues when my shoes are worn out. It's something I've dealt with since high school, but this time around, I had just attributed it to getting older. Almost instantly after putting new shoes on, the problem seem to go away.

What does this example have to do with the poem? The lower back pain reminded me of a paper cut. I ignored my lower back pain for months, because it wasn't bad, and I was able to continue exercising. Although it was painful when I got done exercising, I lived with it. But one easy choice - getting new shoes - solved the problem easily.

I compared this to my walk with the Lord. I've had times where a little sin crept back in, before long, and the little cut required more attention. Anxiety is something I hand over to the Lord, the ultimate doctor. I'd rather be infected, with God in my soul, than allowing sin to continue to infect my soul. When you receive God's love and grace, there is nothing better to help you heal.

Day 18—Light

Scripture

John 8:12, Genesis 1:3-5

Poem

In the beginning, there was nothing
A void, the absence of anything

(Genesis 1:3-5) *3 Then God said,* (NASB)
"Let there be light; and there was light.

4 God saw that the light was good;
and God separated the light from the darkness.

5 God called the light day, and the darkness
He called night. And there was evening
and there was morning, one day."

Light highlights all of creation
God's great handy work

Darkness is the opposite
Darkness is a void, nothing

You can't explain it
People just know the difference

One moment you see clearly
The next moment, you can't

In a blink, Light returns
Darkness is no longer present

Darkness can remain in the shadows
Only because Light allows it

People have free will
They can choose their own path

One leads to Light
The other leads to Darkness

In a broken world, things happen
They can't be explained

Each of us are God's owns Lights of the world
Created to shine in his image

Some of the Lights shine for a while
Some not very long

When someone's Light goes before their time
It leaves a void, darkness in our heart

We yearn for them, much like the Light.
"God, we pray for those who Light goes before they should

We pray for those left behind
Trying to find their Light again, amongst the darkness

Jesus, thank you for being the Light of the world
On this side of heaven. There is plenty of darkness.

One day, we'll just see the Light
Our Father's Light shining for all eternity.

Until then, we hold out hope
The Light of the world will return one day!"

Amen!

Story Behind the Poem

I was driving to work one day and the morning sunrise was
happening. As light appeared over the horizon, darkness retreated.

At that moment, I realized how comforting light is. Darkness makes people uncomfortable and scared. As the saying goes, "things go bump in the night."

I had the thought one day that all things we did will come to light; you won't be able to hide them in darkness. It can be a negative thought, a glance where you shouldn't, or just a sharp tone. All things will come out! If you don't have Jesus standing next to you, you may spend an eternity in darkness and the absence of God for a long time. That is something I don't want to imagine.

Secondly, there was a news story this past year about a gunman killing more than 20 people in Connecticut, and many were young kids. I don't know why their light was extinguished before their time. My heart yearns for those left behind, to deal with the darkness that happened that day.

Our only true hope is to believe in the Light of the world, Jesus. Many will ignore or reject him, but he will help us through things like this. Although we can't explain it, it's simple: you can choose Light or darkness. I chose Light!

Day 19—Little Lost Sheep

Scripture

Matthew 18:12-14

Poem

There was once a herd of sheep
They had been moving from field to field

Grazing, day in and day out
This had been going on for a while

One day, the Shepherd protecting them
Asked them to go to a new place

"The place is so special, the grass is greener
The hillsides are beautiful, the landscape is breathtaking."

As they were getting ready to go
One little sheep stumbled and was unable to make the journey

The Shepherd was very sad not all his sheep could go.
To protect the rest of the sheep, the one could not make the trip

The little hurt sheep stayed back in the old field
Which was safe and sound, yet the little sheep was alone.

Although the sheep was yearning to go to with the rest
Fences were put up blocking his path.

After much prayer and yearning
The Holy Shepherd made things right.

The little sheep, feeling abandoned at first
Was not abandoned by the Holy Shepherd.

He got the sheep

To the very special place with the others

When the little sheep rejoined the rest of his friends
He was so happy just to be there

Although we can't understand why this happened
In the bigger picture, the little sheep will eventually know.

The Holy Shepherd keeps track of his flock
No matter the circumstance, no matter the trial

The next time you are facing a problem
Please ask for help from your Holy Shepherd

He'll guide you through trial and ruin
He'll guide you to the special place, forever!

Amen!

Story Behind the Poem

I was on a plane heading to Israel and we were minutes from taking off when a lady walked up crying. The flight attendant was instructing the person that she had to get off the plane. She was about to sit down in her seat when some luggage fell and hit her in the back of the head. It caused a headache, and the airline was concerned about someone making a trans-Atlantic flight with a potential closed head injury. The bad thing was that the airline left them alone at the airport and didn't follow up any further. Fortunately, she was able to get on the next flight, and only missed a day and a half of the trip.

When she finally arrived in Israel, she was grateful just to make the trip. She waited 20 years to come. We were in Bethlehem shopping for souvenirs at the time, so I suggested they should get a little sheep as a reminder. She was our little lost sheep and fit the story in Matthew 18:12 (NASB): "What do you think? If any man has a hundred sheep, and one of them has gone astray, does he not leave the ninety-nine on the mountains and go and search for the one that is straying?"

The Bible mentions Jesus will never leave us, no matter the circumstance. This can be comforting during times of trial. Although we didn't find out why she was meant to miss a day and a half in Israel, she was grateful to make the rest of the trip.

✝

Day 20—Live and Let Live

Scripture

1 Peter 3:8-22

Poem

They mock, they ridicule
They state only facts will do

Even if God showed himself to these non-believers
They would probably doubt his existence

They doubt, even though science was invented by the Creator
Scripture states they need faith.

If they can't believe in what they can see,
How can we believe in something they can't?

The world is one amazing miracle
People are another miracle

Why can't people acknowledge that?
The last few years have been amazing

I've come to realize my faults and that
I can't handle the world alone

A wise person told me they are actually impressed
By the fact people are willing to handle the world themselves

The world as we know it is falling apart
Morals from generations past have failed to stay intact

People wanting independence, thinking they are smarter than they
really are
Not sure if it's pride, or foolishness, or what

All I know is that my heart hurts
Because the non-believers give no credence to anyone who
believes differently

All they can do is put people down, stating facts are needed
I respect the need for facts

Heck, even a former preacher became one of the leaders
Of the non-believer movement!

Not sure what happened in his life to become so bitter
towards believers
He probably would make me look foolish

All I have is my own testimony
If a person tries to rebuke that, they are a bigger fool than
they realize

I must learn to have grace and move on
The enemy wants us to get in the trenches and argue

When we know the outcome will be different.
I, for one, have faith in God

He shows up daily in my life
Where it's headed, I don't know.
"I have a plan for you," he stated long ago.

The anxiety is still a little there
Although I know different

"I thank the two doubters I read about for inspiring this poem
I hope to be better prepared for future doubters.

To let live and let live
Not get caught up in the mud, which does nothing but get us dirty

Thank you Lord for showing up in my life

I pray for the rest of mankind!"

Amen!

Story Behind the Poem

This poem was inspired by a couple of people who were ranting on an online posting about the NFL player Tim Tebow, and his book. I got into some back and forth discussion; it created some anxiety on my side, which I know I'm open to, when I respond to non-believers. In Romans 12:17 (NASB): "Never pay back evil for evil to anyone. Respect what is right in the sight of all men." When the moment had passed, I remembered this scripture.

I can't change anyone's mind, let alone a person who does not believe in Jesus. It causes me and my heart to feel for these people, for they lack the experience of having the Creator talk to them to impact their life in a positive, constructive way. If this was another world religion(s), they wouldn't be nearly as open to criticize. Only when it comes to Jesus, do people feel they can put the Creator down.

Day 21—Outlook

Scripture

Acts 7

Poem

There are those who see things
With the glass half full

There are those who see things
With the glass half empty

Depending on which side you believe
Describes your outlook

In our world today, people often react before thinking
With all the distractions, compromise is impossible

A majority do not believe in the Bible as truth
We are left to our own vices to work out our "personal truth"

I once knew a person who wanted to be physically fit
Someone young, with lots of potential

They asked for some assistance
Their loved ones bought them equipment

Their opinion was "You'll use it for a short time."
But to this very day, the passion is still there

Another person I once knew
Was full of life, enjoyed many outdoor activities

Then tragedy struck, a life-changing course happened
But they just rolled their sleeves up, learned different things

Even though their new activities were different

Their attitude and outlook remained the same

Our Savior and many of his followers in the Bible
Conveyed this outlook on life

Even Stephen, who was witness to the truth
Caused those in authority to gnash their teeth

They didn't want to hear the truth, much like today
He saw the glory of God

With Jesus at the right hand
His outlook was forward

Not letting the worries of the day get him down.
The next time you get down, the enemy will think he is
making inroads

Remember Stephen's example
Even though things were grim for him

His outlook was upwards, towards heaven
Not on the problem of the day!

For believers - hang in there
Although things may look dim today,

Remember to have an eternal outlook
This should help brighten your day.

Knowing you have eternal salvation
With our Lord and Savior Christ Jesus.

Amen!

Story Behind the Poem

I met a couple of retired people who had distinctly different
stories, but their outlook on life was very positive. Their stories

were separate journeys, yet their attitudes remained upbeat and positive regardless of what challenged they encountered. One of them was involved in a car accident, and paralyzed from the waist down; the other has a physical condition that caused people to be unkind to him in his younger years. Despite these obstacles, they are models of maintaining a positive outlook on everyday life.

I'm learning as you get older, your outlook changes, and you don't get so frustrated about things or take them personally. Some would call that perspective, some would call it experience. It's easy to be positive when something is good happening. It's another thing to be positive when something tests you – that's when you see your true outlook or attitude.

Recently when I was facing a tough day, I read Acts 7 and realized that when Stephen told his story to the Sanhedrin, they became furious and stoned him. During this time, instead of panicking, he looked upwards, saw the glory of God, and was at peace. It was a God moment for me personally; something I needed at the time.

Take an inventory of how you react to things in the long term. A majority of the people in our society now don't attend church regularly, which causes them to avoid actively living what the Bible has to say. The news especially impacts me negatively, and affects my outlook. I'm sure it does that for others, too. Our world today wants answers now, feedback now, with no thought of the future. If you continually seek the here and now, God will wait until you adjust your outlook, or fall on your face from failure. He might also let that happen, so you can be of use to Him.

Day 22—Peaceful Servant

Scripture

Psalm 23, 35

Poem

Ever been to a place where time forgot
Beautifully modern, yet so peaceful

Masterworks of art everywhere
Including the name of our Lord and Savior, Jesus

Lots of crosses, books and pictures
One of kinds items there too

Quality made, with values long since gone
When you view them, you know they are good

The serene view is breathtaking
The water is calm, not a ripple

Everywhere is God's handiwork
The workers are just here to assist

God is in charge of every detail
You can sense his presence

When you are a servant of God
You desire nothing but his love

The calm you feel is almost surreal
The stresses of the day just slip away

You just sit about for a while
Talking with friends and family
You reconnect with them, and the batteries are recharged

At the same time, the Holy Spirit is hovering

His presence assists us on Earth
Providing peace and guidance

When you connect with God and do his work
Your soul becomes so peaceful

Stresses, problems and troubles
Slip away hope to never return

Thank you God, for spots like this
Where we can connect with you, family and friends

One day we'll stand in heaven in your presence
Enjoying your eternal peace and wonders!

Amen!

Story Behind the Poem

I wrote this story while spending a weekend getaway with my wife, family and friends. We went to a place called The Shack, which is anything but a 'shack'; it's a beautiful place in Jugville, Michigan. The place is run by an old couple in their 80s or 90s, who serve free ice cream every night, scooping it by hand. God truly blessed this couple and their ministry. To have a multi-million-dollar log cabin-style getaway located in the middle of a small town is incredible.

My wife and I went for just one night; it was a VERY calming experience. There is nothing else in this town where The Shack resides. Maybe that's why it's so restful – there's little stimulation or distractions. One of the unique things is they have a small one-building museum. There were really old cars that were in perfect condition, old farm equipment and other antiques on display.
If you ever have a chance to visit there, I strongly encourage it!
You'll walk away refreshed, with a new perspective.

In a book that challenges you to do things uncomfortable on purpose, this story is an example of how to get away to be refreshed, to handle uncomfortable things in a Godly way.

✝

Day 23—Petty

Scripture

James 1:27

Poem

Things in life come and go
There are hills and valleys

Highs and lows
Commitment seems impossible
When the challenges keep coming

The good times quickly evaporate
Strife and frustration remain

There are so many bigger things in life
Cancer, stress, uncertainty and fear

When petty things crop up
It makes you feel bad that you're even upset

But petty things can fester
The enemy sits back and waits

He uses negative emotions to further his mission
To destroy, conquer and devour you

Petty feelings are only temporary
The effects linger on

It is Biblical to express concern, and sin directly
With your brother
Get it over quickly and move on

The enemy does not need much to move in
He uses petty feelings against us

Jesus was the ultimate role model
His parables provide direction

It doesn't matter what situation
His Word is always right

Jesus, thank you for being there
In the best of times, and the darkest of times

I ask for repentance and forgiveness
I ask for your grace and mercy

Help me get over the petty feelings
Help me get back on track

Help me be a Kingdom seeker
Help me be a Kingdom bringer

Focus on what matters!

Amen!

Story Behind the Poem

Bad things happen — to everyone. It seems so much of our time can be focused on the negative portion of an experience. But we need to keep all of life's experiences in perspective.

When we let little things impact us, a lot of damage can be done. This damage can take years, even a lifetime to overcome, when in hindsight, we might have blown the situation out of proportion. Every time you are around people who are negative, the situation you're in can linger and impact our ability to have a positive relationship with God. Although this could be temporary, the effects could be longer term.

I'm still learning not to let little things affect my life. The enemy uses these against us, I believe. Negativity is a bad habit that and won't let you move forward. I encourage myself to let things go and look ahead. Let the past go, live in the here and now, and do your best to leave the future in God's hands. When we focus on others and how you can help them, you'll reflect on others and let the petty things go.

†

Day 24—Prayer

Scripture

Matthew 17:20, 6:24

Poem

Lord, I come to you in two ways
To express my own despair about our world and the impact it has
on me

And I come to you for the same reason, on the world's behalf.
In both cases, only you can fix it.

I read an article that started out hopefully,
But mostly expresses despair

I read another headline
About last minute scrambling

Yet another headline
It ended in death

In all three examples
No hope, only despair

Other headlines are about religion:
"Let's take God out of the public eye"

I know religion is man-made,
Rules that men try to live up to and fail

Why does man think they know best
They claim to be wise
Yet when left to their own devices

All that is left are
Sharp divisions among men

The only thing that seems to solve problems is money
And there is not enough to go around

As your Word states, Lord, you can't serve two masters
You'll love one and despise the other

It is *so* depressing when reading the news
It impacts me so deeply, words can't describe it

I still wonder how these words help others
I'm sure one day you'll reveal that to me

My heart grows hard reading news written by men
It makes you want to crawl into a cave and hibernate until the
second coming

War here, poverty there, lack of resources everywhere
Only a few seem to have enough, and that isn't enough for them

How can we protect our eyes from such despair
How can we protect our hearts from such hopelessness

There is a small glimmer of hope
That tells me things will get better

The world offers only temporary relief
From such an unbalance

I know the world will never be at peace
When they don't acknowledge the true peace

When so many want it their own way
No way is the only way that happens

No progress, no peace, no satisfaction
My heart yearns to hand over ALL of this dissatisfaction to you

Prayer is a gift from you
I know from first-hand experience that it works

In all cases, big and small
We have to hand over all

Let you resolve in your own time
We need patience and forgiveness

The last few weeks, a lot has happened
In the next weeks, a lot will happen

If I don't regularly have a conversation with you
The hopelessness I feel will return

I pray for you to remain active in our world and mine
When this happens, all other things are just details

Things seem to just work themselves out
I'm not quite sure how, it just does

I pray for those who don't understand how this works
I pray for those who don't think to pray

I pray for those who haven't experienced the joy prayer brings
I pray for those who don't acknowledge you

I know you, yet my heart wants to be selfish
Prayer is a great mystery; prayer works, so give it time

I end how I began. I pray for two things
I pray for the ability to hand despair over to you

Our world realizes it doesn't know best
And will wake up and realize that you don't always learn from the
past

You are doomed to repeat it.
We are headed down that path

A mustard seed of hope will go a long ways

Our world could use a jar of that today and beyond.

Amen!

Story Behind the Poem

Keeping up with change is challenging sometimes. I know; I work in IT (Information Technology). One day the next version of an operating system came out. There were divisions among those who wanted things to remain the same; they criticized the change. But eventually you need to adopt the next technology.

If you talk to some non-believers, they talk science; "Prove this" and "Prove that," they say. I challenge them to try something new - try prayer on for size, I say. Most don't take me up on it. I think they're partly afraid that it'll work!

On this side of Heaven, I'm impacted daily with the negativity and drama-driven world we live in. I tend to lose hope sometimes. I also have to remember with all of the media and other evil we see around us, to protect my eyes and, more importantly, my heart. If left unattended, the hopelessness gets in, and could ruin any sense of normalcy. When things are "off," and we're in the midst of change, despair sees an open window to our hearts and tries to get in. But things seem to resolve themselves when we honestly hand them over to God. I've experienced this first-hand, and no one can convince me otherwise.

For example, my wife and I were out shopping one day, and she showed me a necklace that had a mustard seed in it. This was another sign God uses everyday things to help me write these stories; in this example, a mustard seed.

Day 25—Reflection

Scripture

John 3:16, Exodus: 20, Matthew 22:34-40

Poem

Waking up one morning next to the lake
The water is as still as glass

A mountain in the background
The reflection of it shadows on the water perfectly

Sitting on the porch
Drinking coffee in the morning

Pondering what is ahead for that day
Or thinking of problems overcome

Rocking back and forth in
Trying to muster enough energy to get around for the day.

No TV, no Internet, no radio, no noise
Just sitting in the swing, listening to God's creation

A deep breath is taken
This seems so perfect, so simple, why don't we seek this
more often?

We hop on the highway of life
One problem after another, one distraction after another

Days, weeks, months, years go by
We get in the routine of hustle and bustle

Forgetting the time of simple, calm ways
We long for this and when we attempt to slow down

Our mind is still in the fast lane, thinking of life's problems
and distractions
The small still voice is trying to get through all the clutter

Sitting on the porch
The small still voice can be heard loud and clear

In the hustle of everyday life
Our idols, problems, distractions all take a higher priority

Only when something stops us, abruptly, like
A death, the loss of a job, or some other impactful situation

It forces us to stop and take a breath from the pace of life
The enemy uses distraction as one of their tools to take our focus
off the Creator

The greatest commandment mentions we shall give our mind,
hearts and attention to God
Not a portion - all of them

Being distracted by the world isn't necessarily a bad thing
It's when you put the world before God, that it can be dangerous

Where are you at in your walk with the creator?
Do you have idols? Do you have habits you can't give up?

Take a moment to reflect, or unplug as the iGeneration calls it
See who and what you are really focusing your attention on...
who you are watching

If you are worried about others' business
And need to check on what others are doing

Worried about what they think of you
Or feel the need to check in all the time

Take a break
Read the Greatest Commandment, and ask for guidance!

It will feel awkward, and probably uncomfortable
The feeling will quickly pass

It'll put you back to Him, when you can see reflections of the mountain in the water
The creator's small still voice providing guidance.

Amen!

Story Behind the Poem

I woke up one morning thinking of all kinds of negative things. I was worried about several things, some about home, a couple from work and some personal items.

I was also reading a story of a person who is a reporter for a popular website. They tried to unplug for five days, failed miserably, and gave in before the five days was done. They traveled to a resort in the Caribbean, but after a few days, they had to check email. They couldn't stand it! The first thing that came to my mind was "You shall have no other idols before me."

It amazes me how self-absorbed the iGeneration has become, and how weak humans get addicted to other peoples' attention. We are all vulnerable to this happening. Working in technology, I can relate wanting to "keep in touch," even while not at work. But this is not where God wants our focus.

Day 26—Rush

Scripture

Luke 18:1–7, Romans 2:7

Poem

Have you ever had the feeling
You go and go and go

And wonder if the merry-go-around of life will ever stop?
You chase after this problem and that problem

Hoping the to-do list will be emptied
This rushed feeling can be especially felt during the holidays

You have this person to shop for
That gift to pick up

I don't have the money
But I'll charge it and pay it off later

Before long, you have three or four cards
Charged to the max with different amounts

On one hand, you feel relief
The shopping list is complete

On the other hand, you feel anxiety
The debt incurred is more than you anticipated
Then you are distracted again.

We do not stop, even for a second, to reflect anymore.
In the days gone by, life was slower, more even-paced.

I wonder if those days will ever come back?
THEN I am reminded: God's Word slows us down.
It has been only seven days since I last went to church.

It only takes seven days to get
This crazy, anxiety-filled, impatient, negative train of thought back.

What is it like for those who regularly don't read God's word
And don't fellowship with other believers?

Their thoughts must be a whole lot worse
God's words are so clear, so refreshing, and bring hope.

For those who say the Old Testament words are negative,
I can relate and understand... until you know the story
behind them.

I am glad the Holy Spirit reminded me where hope comes from:
The WORD of God.

Amen!

Story Behind the Poem

I had missed a week of church at one point; I don't recall the
reason why. Life was busy as usual, and I was doing all kinds of
things. Also, during this time, I wasn't reading the Bible on a daily
basis. There was pressure to complete everyday tasks. My
thoughts began to turn negative. I was surprised how fast my old
habits returned. When I was putting this manuscript together,
parts of the story were inspired during the holidays of 2012. It was
then that I had a little downtime. It made me take some time off
to spend with the family and spend time with our Creator.

Christmas shopping these days is portrayed by the media so early;
in the fall season, and before other traditional holidays. The
atmosphere now is that you have to get this and that; and they
push you to think that you don't have a lot of time. When Jesus
was born, simple gifts were brought. They were humble and meant
a lot. Getting back to the simpler and more meaningful holiday is
what I strive for.

SECTION 3 – Spear

Uncomfortable Testimony by Scott Forsyth

One area in my life that makes me uncomfortable is public speaking. I have many opportunities for training and public speaking in both technical and Biblical roles, and I know that God has called me as a teacher and speaker, but it has never been easy for me. Every time I have a speaking engagement, the weight of it sits on my shoulders for days or weeks in advance, leaving a nagging feeling that sticks with me. However, I know that God has called me to it, and he has blessed me with the ability to do well as a trainer and speaker.

I know that I need to continue to pursue these opportunities, even though they are one of the most undesirable tasks that I do. After speaking engagements, however, I am usually greatly energized and thankful for the opportunity. This is what keeps me going for the next time.

When we are uncomfortable with areas in our lives, we need to prayerfully ask ourselves if it is because it's wrong for us, or if it's right, and if God is purposefully stretching us. There is an important difference, and if an uncomfortable area is not from God, do what you can to delegate or avoid that area in your life. However, if it is from God, then pursue it with all of your heart, because God will use it in a powerful way in your life. He is preparing you for greatness.

- Scott Forsyth

Day 27—Scared

Mark 9:14-29

Poem

Tightness in the chest
Fear of having a heart attack

It is a natural feeling of the unknown
To be scared of something we do not control

Of all feelings God created
Scared ranks right up there at the top of the list

Have a hard task at work?
Out of your comfort zone?

Do you get nervous on the big stage?
When the tough starts happening, do you start happening?

Or do you get scared
And get nervous that you'll fail

Scared is the first cousin of fear
Scared is also doubt and excitement

The enemy exploits us when we're scared
The enemy uses being scared to make us doubt God

"You are not perfect
You are not worthy of His love

You might as well give up
Because you'll never be good enough"

God created scared to heighten our senses

When something bad is around, it's a feeling that protects us

It was not used to create doubt
It was not used to raise fear

God wants us to have a healthy fear of Him
He can erase us from existence with one breath

He can step in and out of time
He works all things for good

I have a healthy respect and fear for God
I know he is there and helping along

Am I scared to meet my maker?
According to his Word, if you accept his son Jesus

You get to spend eternity with Him
It still causes a slight twinge in my chest

Because once you walk from today into eternity
Most likely, you aren't coming back

Your one shot to do your best is gone
So be scared! Use the healthy feelings scared creates

To do God's work on this side of Heaven
Would you rather be scared of mankind or God?

I chose God.

Amen!

Story Behind the Poem

There are verses in the Bible about fearing God. It's not like fearing something on Earth. I can't quite describe it, but maybe it's more of a healthy respect. As a person ages, they finally realize they aren't in control, which can be disturbing. The Bible says not to worry. That is hard; I'll admit there are some things that make me worry. But I try quickly to hand them over to God.

The world today is seeking instant gratification. These days, people use social media to share their feelings and observations, with little fear. God is the final judge; we all have to face Him. I both fear the good Lord as well as respect Him. He has revealed himself to me, and the journey has just begun. Keeping a healthy dose of fear of the Lord helps keep things in perspective.

✝

Day 28—Scars

Scripture

Matthew 11:25-30

Poem

Scars can be little
Scars can be large

People see scars and wonder what happened
Some come from burns, some from car accidents

Scars can be a scrape on a car
Scars can be on a person's body

There are mental scars
The mental ones can linger for a long time

Other scars are self-inflicted
No matter what, they deform the original design

Scars impact everything we do
They make us think twice

They hang around, reminding us of pain
The pain could have been temporary

But if you hang onto the scar
The pain will continue impacting you

The enemy likes scars
They build up and become a burden over time

The former perfect design is now damaged goods
Some things can be replaced

Mental scars don't heal so easily

These require forgiveness, obedience

When Jesus had the nails put into his body
He'd have those scars for all time

Wow, Eternity with Scars!
He didn't have to do this, but he did because he loved us

So whatever the scar, mental or physical,
The sooner you learn to forgive

The sooner you learn to move past the pain
Give it ALL to God and let him handle it

Scars, they deform, they alter, they damage
How you deal with them is between you and the Creator

God, I give you my scars to heal in your own special way
Thank you for being the ultimate scar healer!

Amen!

Story Behind the Poem

I was driving one day and I realized I was hanging onto some things
that were bothering me, and needed to let them go. I was dealing
with a few things that seemed to linger. Some of them were how I
perceived other people, which impacted my perception and mood.

We are social by nature. Sometimes when I'm around others for
extended period of time, it can affect my judgment. Little things
add up over time.

It seems like it would be simple to recognize when you are hanging
onto things, taking a moment to realize it is the biggest thing.
It took me a few years, but it is one more thing I can hand over to
God to handle, because now I know I can't handle it alone.

Day 29—Score

Scripture

1 Corinthians 13:4-7, Mark 12:30-31

Poem

Games keep score to determine who won
It is a basic concept

Whatever the sport, whatever the goal
Have more than your opponent

When you win, you feel good
When you lose, you don't

The cycle repeats
New opponent, same goal

When someone focuses on winning
And does not focus on perfecting their skill

They become frustrated, they become weak
Winning is all that matters

Nothing will satisfy the want to win
The more you want something, the more you try

In life, we keep score
When someone feels like they are wronged

Frustration, dislike and then downright hatred
These feelings can crop up

The enemy loves when this happens
He is just waiting for the chance to pounce

He is just waiting to offer suggestions

"Hate that person, they do not like you

They have it out for you
They do not care about you"

These suggestions enter the mix
And over time, you can come to believe

These negative thoughts and make stuff up
The thoughts might not be true, but they are there

God keeps score too
We wronged him the day we entered the world

We are covered in sin, separated from him
He states He loves us

Love does not keep score
Love does not hate

Love is kind, gentle, uplifting
It is not competitive

When someone wrongs you
Remember what God did for you
Sent his son Jesus to die on a cross for you

That act alone is Love
The two great commandments are about love

When you harbor hate, or wrongful feelings
You contribute to the person who pounded nails into Jesus

These are the sins he took on for us
Don't contribute to hate, it'll do nothing but cause destruction

God doesn't want that
Because he loves you, more than you know.

Amen!

Story Behind the Poem

In the US and abroad, games provide a distraction from everyday life. Fans wear their favorite jersey, and take pride in being a fan of their team. I like sports and the lessons it can teach you about life. American football is my favorite.

However, when all people do is focus on winning, and not the effort behind that it takes to win, you will always lose. One of my high school coaches told me, "Block, tackle, and perform your assignment to the best of your ability; the winning will take care of itself."

That is true in life, too. If all you want to do is have a relationship, but you're not willing to put forth effort, it won't go far. When you are so worried about yourself, you don't think of others. In life, try not to keep score of things done to you, because it's a lot better on your mental and physical health.

Day 30—Sharp

Scripture

Matthew 18:21-35

Poem

Sharp knives cut through almost anything
Words can be so sharp
They can be as bad as knives

Words that show no compassion
Can be expressed in such a tone
They can cause mental scars for a lifetime

"You cannot do this, you cannot do that
You will not succeed, you should not even try"

Then the naysayers pile on
Shouting their sharp negative comments

If you try to make everyone happy
You will succeed in making no one happy
The crowd will have some sharp words

Rarely can people share compassionate words
Like LOVE and RESPECT

There are people who can express their feelings
In soft, respectful and positive tones

Jesus stated to Peter, "How often should I forgive?"
7 x 70 times is a start

To better explain it, completely forgive
If you don't have anything nice to say, don't say it
Our world online today is full of sharp words

Lord, I pray our world finds compassion
Lord, I pray our world finds love

Lord, I pray the only sharp thing
Is someone who is trying to make me a better follower.

Amen!

Story Behind the Poem

I read most of my news, sports and information on the Internet.
I was observing that online comments can be very direct and
mostly negative. It seems when dealing with a text-based society,
people can't discuss things effectively in person anymore.

As with other stories, this inspired all kinds of poems. By nature,
I'm a direct person; other stories have covered this in more detail.
I like to engage in debate, although it won't convince anyone.
I have to be careful not to be sharp.

It's a struggle on a daily basis not to say the first thing that comes
to my mind. The words can be sharp, which have a chance to make
an impression for a lifetime. God's words are honest, and to those
who don't follow him, they can seem negative and sharp.

Once you accept Jesus as your savior, his words show love. I saw a
recent comment by James Watkins (www.jameswatkins.com):
"I don't hate you because I disagree with you; I just love you too
much to agree with you." This is how I feel sometimes; I'll continue
to do my best and not be too sharp.

Day 31—The Days After

Scripture:

James 5:16

Poem

You wake up one day, knowing things should be different
You accept the calling from our Lord and Savior

For a while the emotions are awesome
The feelings are so natural

You didn't realize a person could feel this way
It is a new world

You join groups, dig into His Word and start down the right path
This path has you growing closer to the Father

The day after, a few weeks, or months go by
The old life and some things continue to be the same

Some people haven't adjusted
And consequences from previous decisions remain

Your new-found faith provides some protection
Although the old habits don't go away completely

They try to pull you back to your old self
You resist and pray the problems will disappear

With so much going on, it's hard to keep it straight
Forgiveness is an easy thing to say, although not so easy to
implement at first

The negative emotions of defensiveness come charging back
Before accepting Christ, this was the only way you knew
The enemy sits back and waits to see how we respond

Waiting for the "high" to subside

When things return to normal
When old habits try to creep back in

The enemy will pounce like a roaring lion
Waiting to devour those who recently gave their life to Christ

The old form seems normal and the new normal seems odd
For every individual, their walk and healing their wounds is
different, it takes time

The one thing that is the same is that Jesus is in each of us
The Holy Spirit is there, helping, although we have to choose
to change

In His time, things will smooth out ... although that can seem like
an eternity
Pray and involve those who can help you through it

Sharing your pain with a brother or sister in Christ is a first step
The rage and confusion you feel don't easily go away, nor do
the problems
Plainly state you have changed and that you're trying to live
differently than before

These are difficult things = facing them alone can make
us defensive
When difficult times arise, we need to seek God's help

We need His guidance, direction and love
God, please help new believers to stay on the right path

Towards a stronger relationship with you
Through your son, Jesus Christ!

Amen!

Story Behind the Poem

This story is inspired after observing individuals who recently accepted Christ as their Savior. After the emotional high subsides, trying to live a new life can be hard!

My heart goes out to individuals who are trying to change. The world doesn't make it easy for someone to change. The situations from past decisions remain when we accept Christ. How we work with our past decisions is up to us. We can hand them over to God and seek His guidance.

It's not easy for an adult to change, let along be a Christian, in this day and age. All we can do is have hope in our Savior and what he did for us.

✝

Day 32—Thief

Scripture

Luke 23:32:43

Poem

There once was a man
Who did bad things his whole life

He was tried, convicted and nailed to a cross
He wasn't a lifelong Christian

He hadn't helped anyone
He couldn't even help himself anymore

His only good fortune:
He was nailed up next to the Son of God

He happened to have a change of heart at the right time
He uttered some simple words

They included "Lord, remember me."
The Lord could have ignored this man

He was involved in his own troubles
He had been beaten, battered, and nailed to a cross too
He was bearing all of man's sins, for all time

Just think, the Lord in this very moment
Suffering more than anyone has ever suffered

Had the awareness to pay attention to this thief
He showed love to someone who was getting what he deserved

The Lord didn't condemn him
He forgave him and said in such a way

"You'll be with me in Heaven
You'll be in glory with me forever"

The next time you think someone is beyond saving
The next time you think someone won't listen

Remember the thief, in his final hours
No baptism, no good works, no following Jesus

All he did was call on the Lord with 100% faith
"Lord, I need you in my heart, it's broken

Please, Please, Please I fear God
And want you to help save me."

It's not up to mankind to make judgments of others
It's our Heavenly Father alone

It is never too late while living to call on the name of Jesus
Thank you Christ Jesus for this illustration

Even in your moment of dying,
You were under the most physical, mental and spiritual pain

You took time to save a dying thief
Who had a change in his heart

Thank you, Thank you, and Thank you
For not turning the other cheek; your example provides hope
to us all!

Amen

Story Behind the Poem

I was reading an ebook by D.L. Moody called *Men of the Bible*.
The last story, which was fitting to this section, was the story of
Penitent Thief (Luke 23:32-43). I think unlike any other story, it's
not about works or anything else we can do. The Lord wants your
heart alone, no matter when.

The story made me realize this thief did nothing else, at least covered in the Bible, to earn his way to Heaven. He changed his heart on the cross next to Jesus. This is a great example not to give up on someone; Jesus didn't, and showed forgiveness.

✝

Day 33—Towards Home

Scripture

Romans 5

Poem

Sitting in a rocking chair
Reading a story of brokenness and loss

On the surface, everything was perfect
Money, fame, a nice home and marriage

The world was full of envy
The world was full of praise

Underneath it all was lots of brokenness
Under the cover was insecurity, shame and resentment

There was unfaithfulness, broken promises
The eye wasn't on the prize

It was on other earthly things
And one day the mirror shattered

All the so-called perfection was exposed
They were left standing feeling empty
In one brief moment, God had rebuked everything

God was showing his perfect love
The first step towards coming home

He wants our hearts first
Everything else will come along after that

Things don't happen overnight
Things don't cure themselves quickly

God uses process and patience to help us overcome our
own shortcomings

We try to take control because we don't know his actions
We really try -- only to come to a dead end

We need to fully commit and hand over the wheel
To give God control of our lives

When this happens
Words can't describe the feeling, all we know it's very comforting

God breaks us down
To later build us up for His glory

The more we seek him
The more our lives are filled with His love

A love that can only come from him
All we need is Jesus

His Son showed us the way, we just need to follow
The world won't back away easily

Every day will bring trials
There will be many ups and downs

Only when we don't stray from him, stay with him
Focus our efforts towards home, God's Heavenly home

Can we fully realize God's love?
One day, he will call us Home, his Home!

Amen!

Story Behind the Poem

This poem is inspired by reading *The Road Home* by Denise Jackson,
a book my wife got me for Christmas. The author explained in the

book that her life was built around her husband as the foundation of her life, instead of Jesus. God assisted Denise and Alan to focus their hearts where they needed to be, towards God's home.

It got me thinking about life will be after my sons grow up. It almost brings me to tears just thinking of the moment where the house is empty! God's very presence is overwhelming; He can even take someone who is terse, impatient, and indifferent, and use it for his Glory.

We've known several couples in the past who have split up. After a time, some of them want to reconcile, yet they don't know how. My heart goes out to them. I have this deep desire to help, but I know I can't force my will on them. I want everyone to point their hearts towards home, God's home, because I know this will heal their pain.

✝

Day 34—Trust

Scripture

Exodus 20:16, Luke 16:10, Proverbs 11:3, Romans 12:3, 1 Timothy 1:19, Proverbs 12:5

Poem

Trusting a little is easy
Not revealing the whole truth is easy

Easy becomes safe
People like safe

Safe is comforting to the soul
People feel good when they are safe

When people are uncomfortable
They don't trust

They try to become comfortable again
Some spend their whole life looking for trust

Once trust is broken
It is hard to get back

There are many ways to break someone's trust
One of the ways is to lie

Not telling the whole truth is lying
How can you trust someone

If they don't tell the whole truth?
When you are not around

They tell the other parts they were holding inside
To a group of others, who in turn, spread gossip

Once gossip starts, the heart's true deceit is revealed
People like to talk

But honest conversation is difficult
As people form attitudes and opinions

When this happens, people have to really examine their hearts
They need to look at their inner self

They need to remember who to trust
Men and women will let you down.

When someone lets you down, it's hard to trust again
Trust is a fragile thing

Through trials and tribulations, trust can be formed and
strengthened
When you find a small group to share your life with

Trust can be nurtured and bonds are made
Trust, honesty, integrity are foundations of a relationship

So remember that trust isn't necessarily earned from the start
As when accepting Jesus as your Savior

You know you want something different
Unlearning your old ways and trusting Him takes time

Like accepting others in a group
Trust will come as long as you examine your own heart's intentions

Don't be afraid to be honest, as long as it's to build up, not to
tear down
This is where a person can really start to trust.

Amen!

Story Behind the Poem

I was spending the weekend with my family, and through various conversations and prayer for our small group, the word TRUST came to my heart; so did LOVE. I prayed for guidance on how to start the small group. My Dad and I both expressed that judgment towards others is something we struggled with. It was the same weekend the word TRUST was laid on my heart.

I examined my own heart, because I struggled with focusing on the negative side of a person and it had festered. We all have crutches that we continue to hold onto, for whatever reason. Letting go of resentment will make room in your life for trust to grow and prosper.

✝

Day 35—Ultimate Janitor

Scripture

Hebrews 10

Poem

Every year Christmas comes
Presents are given

This creates trash and unwanted items
All the wrapping paper and bows get in the way

Combined with all the food that is prepared
Trash abounds and starts to stink

Trash bins overflow, and the trash man comes a day later
So all of the trash hangs around a little longer than normal

Old habits crop up at the New Year
And complacency morphs into sin

God's standards are ignored
Apathy sets in

Anxiety happens, language loosens a little
These feelings are like stinky trash

They stink up our soul
The impulses of bad thoughts cause temporary fear

These thoughts and feelings
Stink up our soul so bad, we can't get rid of them fast enough

How easily we forget the Heavenly peace God provides!
This is where Jesus comes in, he is willing to take out our trash

He provides grace and mercy
"God, we need daily pickup, please help keep us on track

Help keep the enemy away from our trash
So he can't hold on to it and use it against us."

Jesus is the ultimate janitor
Taking out the trash of our souls.

Amen!

Story Behind the Poem

During the first church service of the New Year, we were singing during the service and when the Pastor said the phrase, "taking out the trash," I was inspired.

I had had a few days off between Christmas and New Year's. My family watched a lot of movies; some probably weren't the best for a Christian. It reminded me I needed to clean up what I watched. These less than Christian movies can impact your walk with Christ.

Regardless of the little things, they were like trash cluttering up my mental life. When we ask Jesus to come into heart, he helps clear our souls of the garbage. The Holy Spirit moves in and starts helping cleaning up our new Christ-centered life.

Day 36—Unforgiveness

Scripture

Matthew 6:14-15

Poem

Ever had someone talk to you negatively?
What was your reaction?

Did it surprise you at first?
You weren't sure how to react?

The first response might have been, did I do something to offend?
You try to be cordial, and if they respond negatively again ...

Later they might be nice enough to help
But their tone is sharp.

Another day, another negative tone ...
They become more blunt

We entered their world unexpectedly
Our actions were prohibiting them from enjoying the moment
Unaware we were impacting this person

Instead of showing compassion, and kindness
Their words were demeaning and intended to show dominance

In other cases, the words don't have to be sharp
They can be vague, hard to understand

Individuals say one thing
But their actions say another
In all cases, when relying on man for support
People will let you down

Their reactions will not be what is expected
The natural response is to take things personally

There are times in life
When you don't know all the answers

You become concerned or confused
When we ask for help and don't wait

Pride rises up
There can be unintended consequences

Feelings are hurt, forgiveness disappears
Division happens, openness fades

I am reminded of our Savior
He was questioned the same way

By blunt authority figures
He simply stated, "I speak the truth."

His words did not judge
His actions were neutral

He did not become defensive
He knew his purpose

He could have called on Heaven's armies
To defend him and his deity

He chose to show restraint
He chose to show forgiveness

When others were not so forgiving
They were selfish, judgmental

The Bible states in Matthew 6:14-15 (NASB)
"14 For if you forgive others for their transgressions,
your Heavenly Father will also forgive you.

15 But if you do not forgive others,
then your Father will not forgive your transgressions."

Those words are clear
Forgive, and you will be forgiven

If you don't, you won't
No matter the case, no matter the situation

We all expect forgiveness
Although holding back forgiveness is man's first reaction

The next time this is directed towards you
Remember the example and words given to us by our creator.

Amen!

Story Behind the Poem

There have been a few situations where I was interacting with others who I didn't know very well. Instead of having a positive, helpful tone in their words, they were blunt, and not very nice. It was almost like I did something to offend them.

There have been a couple of situations where I acted on my own, with the most innocent of intentions; however, my actions went against Biblical examples. Although my intentions were good, I could have caused confusion and strife for others. This is yet another case where God provided an awesome gift, and instead of waiting for the appropriate time to respond in his timing, I tried to take control.

The lesson I learned is to wait for God, and regardless if someone is nice to you or not, be forgiving. Understand that most times it isn't your action that causes another person to be short-tempered or unfriendly; it's most likely something going on in their life. If you do not pay evil for evil, as stated in 1 Peter 3:9 (NASB): "Not returning evil for evil or insult for insult, but giving a blessing instead; for you were called for the very purpose that you might inherit a blessing," you act as our Savior did.

Day 37—Wake-up

Scripture

1 Thessalonians 5:2

Poem

How would you classify yourself when you wake up?
Are you a morning person?

Do you like the stillness of the morning?
The calm before the storm of the day

When your eyes open, your mind starts right away
You are alert, attentive and ready for the day.

If this doesn't sound like you …
Are you more of a night person?

Quiet times after everyone is in bed
You sit around and reflect on the past day
Lay around, read a book to wind down

Your idea of early morning starts about an hour before lunch
There are portions of the morning that you didn't think existed.

Whatever type of person you are
You are unique

What about a country?
Do you think they have morning types?

Or are they more of a night owl?
What does it take to wake a country up?

Regardless of what type of person you are
Eventually you have to wake up and face reality
If you stay in a fog

Eventually, things will get so unorganized

There will be disarray, confusion and blame
"I don't feel good, so it's someone else's problem."

The Bible states that Jesus will return one day
He will come down not as a lamb, but a lion

Not sure about you, but that scares me to death
I want to be ready for that day, and make sure I'm awake

And ready to go home with the King of Kings
His action will be swift, and decisive

If we are not spiritually awake, we could miss it
When we step from Earth into eternity

Make sure you do it with your eyes open
Your mind sharp and awake

You won't want to miss the wonders
That is waiting for us in Heaven!

Amen!

Story Behind the Poem

I believe that the USA is in a fog; it's not quite awake. It's stumbling around like someone who just woke up from a long sleep. We used to be "the early bird gets the worm" sort of country. We were aggressive.

In recent generations, we've gotten caught in a stupor, and suddenly, we are in debt, we've lost our spiritual way, everyone has an opinion but no one wants to hear the truth—no one wants to believe in our past and founding principles.

Surround yourself with a sphere of influence that adheres to your Christian example, before it's too late. Don't find out that Jesus has come like a thief in the night. Eternity is a long time and "sleeping in" could cost you your soul.

†

Day 38—What Do You Need in this World?

Scripture

Revelation 3:14-22

Poem

What do you need in this world?
Good question

The polite Christian answer is Jesus alone (which is true... read on)
Many roll their eyes and go about their merry way

They say you are crazy
And don't know what you are talking about

Here is something to think about:
Do you ever struggle with things?

Do you have situations you don't know how to handle?
Are there times in life when things are overwhelming?

Do you get depressed once in a while?
Do you have worries about this or that?

Wouldn't it be nice to hand your problems, fears and worry to
someone who can handle them?
"Here is my worry; I don't know how to handle this."

Better yet: "I don't know what to do here."
Knowing at the appropriate time the answer will come

Yes, it will take some patience
Think of it as a challenge

The Lord is big enough to handle anything you can hand him
He loves you so much he died for you

Still not convinced?
Ever wonder what's next?

What is beyond this crazy and mixed-up world?
Too scared to think about it?

The two things everyone has in common
Being born and dying, no exceptions

It is scary knowing that some feel they can handle all their
problems on their own.
The next time something good or bad happens

The next time you are faced with something unknown
Try saying, "Jesus, I'm not quite sure here

I don't know even if I believe all this stuff
I'm willing to open my heart and try it out

Please help me in this situation
I don't even have the words to describe it

I've heard you know... even if I don't know how to say it."
Sit back and wait to see how things go

When, and yes, when the prayer is answered
Give credit where credit is due

It might make you feel uncomfortable at first
The answer might not be what you expected

It will be what you needed, though
Then, the next time something comes up

Try it all over again. Say "Jesus,
It's me again. I have this thing I need some assistance on

Can you come along side of me and help out?
I really appreciate your being able to help in areas I can't."

It's real easy to get to know him
He's the one knocking at the door

Just say, "Come on in, Jesus.
Please take over in the driver's seat.

I don't like tackling this crazy world alone
Since I hear you conquered death

I figure you can conquer anything that is in my life."
Before you know it, you'll realize Jesus is all you need!

Amen!

Story Behind the Poem

There have been countless times that I've faced issues that I didn't
know how to solve. The frustration level can get so high, it
practically ruins your day. No matter how you look at it, you have
an almost toxic attitude. Everyone around you can see it in your
body language. The enemy reminds you over and over about
it, trying to win. And you just want to hibernate for the rest of
the day.

I know better. Yet I'll be in the heat of the moment, and forget.
I might have not gotten enough sleep, which of course, will impact
me more. It'll take hours, or days, in some cases, to forget and
move on. Letting go of something negative when you have a
natural passion to solve things, when something isn't quickly
resolved, creates a level of frustration.

In my walk with the Lord, I've had a lot of challenges. I've handed
them over, and then when I almost forget I have the problem
anymore, the solution comes to me. While you're in it, though,
that feeling of relief seems like it'll never arrive. Even though some
might not believe in the power of the Holy Spirit, it's a comforting
feeling knowing you can hand over anything, truly anything, in a
moment of prayer.

Day 39—What Pride Tried to Do

Scripture

John 14:16-31

Poem

My pride hurts when someone else got the glory
I want to let it go and move on.

My mind won't let the thought go
I sit here wondering when the pain will go away

I know better and want the pain to go away
I try to focus on other things
But it keeps cropping up like a weed.

I pray to God that he takes the pain
I get the sense he is teaching me a lesson

I'll be glad he is teaching me this lesson, in the long run
It'll make me a better person

It is not hard to identify the right thing to do
It IS hard to make the right decision and stick with your morals

Read Job 37-41, about the ultimate humbling experience
Having the Creator personally humble you would be quite a sight.

Pride can try to get in the way
You can decide to hang onto it or give it to God

Enjoy the test pain and be glad God is on your side
I don't want any glory if this helps someone else

I want ALL the glory to go to God.
I thank Jesus for dying on the cross

God wants your heart, and to follow him
Having a willing attitude is a first step.

Don't let your pride get in the way
Don't give in, because for pride to win

All it has to do is stick around.
Don't give pride the power it wants!

In the end, God is God and you are not
Give your pride to God.

Amen!

Story Behind the Poem

One day I was feeling pride... but realized I needed to be humble, and I needed God's help. The Holy Spirit helped me remember an important lesson: the story of Job. That left such a powerful impression on me. No matter the situation, circumstance or emotion, there is NOTHING we can do that comes close to God's power. Pride took down the enemy for an eternity.

SECTION 4 – RESULT

Uncomfortable Testimony by Pastor Joel Heron

Doing Hard Things for God: "Quiet & Slow Is Hard"

I am an ENFP. If you've ever taken the Meyers-Briggs Temperament Analysis, then you know ENFP's are the lively, talkative, social bugs of the personality bunch. If there isn't a party to attend, then we're organizing one! I'm also a Wesleyan pastor. I have often said to my congregation, "I have 'preacher disease'— Help! I'm talking and I can't shut up!"'

That said, it is especially hard for me to simply BE QUIET AND SLOW DOWN (see, I even put QUIET and SLOW in ALL CAPS); in fact, it is sometimes hard for me just to BE. When I asked my church leadership and congregation at Greenville Community Church for a sabbatical a few months back, one of the questions amid a bevy of concerns for me was, "Pastor, if you get away for an extended sabbatical, will you really be able to get away and be quiet?" It was a valid question.

I knew this because in times past, I have been able to deny myself the basics of life in order to get closer to God—fasting, as it's called in Christian circles. Yet, here's what I've found: it much easier to deny myself the sweet taste of Coke than the "sweet sights" of the Internet; it is easier for me to give up a meal than to give up a movie. In fact, it is much harder for me to keep my tongue from talking than to keep my tongue from tasting. If you ask what is hard for this active, talkative, frenetic ENFP, I'll respond—in a word—quiet.

I'm on day fourteen of a four-month sabbatical, and it has taken me fourteen days to begin to find a new rhythm, melody and harmony. Compare me to a classical music piece and I would be Wagner's The Ride of the Valkyries *or Tchaikovsky's* 1812 Overture *(especially the end): tempo—allegro, bells—chiming, cymbals—clashing, tympanis—booming, strings—sawing, wind instruments—open-valve. I'm much less likely to be a Chopin nocturne or a Beethoven piano sonata.*

But I've learned something about symphonies that teaches me about a Christ-centered, balanced life. Timeless classical pieces enjoyed by most, all have something in common—a beautiful but simple balance to them. It is a joy to listen to an orchestra like the Boston Symphony or the London Philharmonic play a song with a variety of tempos and dynamics. Consider the following four combinations of tempo and dynamics: allegro[1]/forte[2]*;* allegro/piano[3]*;* adagio[4]/forte*;* adagio/piano*. For you music enthusiasts, there are the "mezzos-" and the "-issimos"; there are the "prestos" and the "moderatos", but for the sake of illustration, here I will land on four combos. They apply to music; they apply to life. (Haven't you noticed that music and life often hold up mirrors to each other?)*

Like noted above, sometimes an orchestra plays allegro/forte*. The composer's arms are flailing the air with jumping jacks tempo and the orchestra is in full wind—all instruments playing. This combination reminds me of a day when I'm in full wind (or fully winded), rushing in and out of meetings where all instruments are talking and there's no silence. Maybe it's a day of putting out fires (real or imagined) and mopping up messes (mine or another's). At the end of a day like that, I fall into a chair or a bed thinking, "O Rest where art thou?" I need to drink in the lilting notes of Chopin's* Nocturne No. 2 in E-flat *on the piano and in* piano*! If you can identify, by all means find a vehicle to help you shift into "N."*

Sometimes an orchestra plays allegro/piano*. In the tune* Peer Gynt in the Hall of the Mountain King*, I can hear the xylophone, oboe and clarinet (in the middle of the piece) with a delicate dynamic but an ever-increasing,* allegro *pace. Although the rest of the orchestra is silent, there are one or two instruments playing at a rapid click.*

This pace/volume combo reminds me of writing a eulogy for a funeral. I'm often under the gun, because the time between a person's death and the time of the funeral is usually only two or three days. Of course, during those hours, there are other things to do as well. But the eulogy must get done. Death doesn't wait and neither do mourners. So, I'm usually in a room, quietly but quickly pecking away at the computer keys (like right now) in order to compose a good word for the deceased. Although things are quiet, the steady pressure of getting done dictates a faster pace than usual. My heart often races, my palms sweat and my blood pressure rises. What are the near-silent, but crucial activities in your life requiring you to quickly get on and get over? Quietly but quickly needs other-side balance too.

Often times an orchestra plays adagio/forte—*slow and stately but loud. In Strauss'* Also Sprach Zarathustra *(Theme from* 2001, A Space Odyssey), *the brass and strings ring out loud, but long, syllables of ever-building sound, yet slowly and majestically. It is a regal tune that sounds as if the prophet, Zarathurstra (Zoroastrianism) is speaking for his god. Like this tune, there are days that require a slower pace, but the full attention of all my faculties. When I work on a long-term project like a sermon series, or a book or a strategic plan, it requires my mind, will and emotions to "play" loudly and forcefully. Although the beat is slow and the gait is walk, the full energy required of all my faculties leaves me almost as spent as "fast and loud." Don't let the slow drain of these heavy projects sneak up on you!*

Finally, there are times when an orchestra plays adagio/piano. *There is a slow, soft solo or duet by one or two instruments that eases the mind and calms the soul, and, quite frankly, readies us for the next rush of rhythm and rage from full orchestra. Think here of the slow violin solo notes at the beginning of* Pachelbel's Canon in D—*slow and soft, like a leisurely stroll through a flower garden. It's quiet and slow; it's relaxing; it's a tune you'd want playing while in a candlelit bubble bath (yes, guys too). That brings me, literally, to*

148

where I am today (day fourteen of a four-month sabbatical). I've been learning about true Sabbath. In his book, The Rest of God, *Mark Buchanan writes about having not only a Sabbath day but also a Sabbath heart. He writes:*

One thing [I]...need to make explicit: when I use the word Sabbath, I mean two things. I mean a day, the seventh day in particular....I want to convince you, in part, that setting apart an entire day, one out of seven, for feasting and resting and worship and play is a gift and not a burden, and neglecting the gift too long will make your soul, like soil never left fallow, hard and dry and spent.

But when I say Sabbath, I also mean an attitude. It is a perspective, an orientation. I mean a Sabbath heart, not just a Sabbath day. A Sabbath heart is restful even in the midst of unrest and upheaval. It is attentive to the presence of God and others even in the welter of much coming and going, rising and falling. It is still and knows God even when mountains fall into the sea. [Cf. Psalm 46]

You will never enter the Sabbath day without the Sabbath heart....I sometimes use the Word Sabbath to refer to both, and sometimes to one or the other. But always my assumption is that both are needed and that each reinforces the other.[5]

Sabbath day? That's an easy one for me. I've been keeping a Sabbath day (with intermittent and sinful inobservances) all my life. Sabbath heart? Admittedly and ashamedly, I don't have a Sabbath heart. Early-morning get-ready-quick-and-out-the-door has been my habit; late-night noise and sensation has been my bedfellow. To put it in musical terms, I tend to work and play at allegro *pace and* forte *volume. I need much more* adagio *and* piano *in life.*

My God and my people, forgive me for not knowing true Sabbath. For, without a Sabbath heart, I haven't kept Sabbath day even though I've faithfully observed it. God grant me more piano: *more quiet mornings with silent sips of coffee and a reading from Thomas Merton under a dew-drenched dawn. God grant me more* adagio: *more stillness and knowledge of the Holy, which go hand in hand according to the Psalmist; more evening prayers through the Psalms and earlier nights without screen or remote.*

And so... a sabbatical, whose purpose is to "slow my roll and quiet my soul," is where I find myself. It has been hard! Putting it another way—it hasn't been easy! Because it is one of the hardest things I will have done, I've had two admonishments from people who care about me that went something like this: "You're taking your phone and computer? You're not getting on Facebook, are you? I thought this was a sabbatical! Go unplug!"

For those of you who, like me, are a whirling dervish (what is that anyway?) in allegro *gear and at* forte *volume, please find Sabbath day(s) with appropriate Sabbath hearts. And by so doing, the* adagio *rhythms and* piano *sounds will bring you a Christ-centered balance. After all, aren't they one and the same: Christ-centeredness and balance?*

---

[1]*Allegro*="fast, quickly and bright", Wikipedia, The Free Encyclopedia.
[2]*Forte*="meaning loud", Wikipedia, The Free Encyclopedia.
[3]*Piano*="meaning soft", Wikipedia, The Free Encyclopedia.
[4]*Adagio*="slow and stately (literally 'at ease')", Wikipedia, The Free Encyclopedia.
[5]Mark Buchanan, *The Rest of God* (Nashville: Thomas Nelson, Inc., 2006), 4.

Day 40—Wounds

Scripture

John 19:16-30

Poem

Wounds can be physical.
Wounds can be mental.

Wounds can be eternal.
Wounds alter the normal.

Wounds alter the original design.
Wounds can be to you.

Wounds can be to other people.
Wounds can change how people perceive.

Wounds can change how people act.
Wounds take many shapes and sizes.

After a while, you believe the negative thoughts, and it feels like an open wound.
Until we face these wounds, in whatever shape they come,
We can't come to grips with those wounds, and heal.

Handing over wounds to Jesus
Is a life-changing experience

When you truly forgive wounds, they hurt no more.
Yes, if they are physical, they are still there.

Jesus shows us that forgiveness is a blessing,
Even though this is NOT easy to do.

When you and Jesus work together,
Wounds become less apparent, and heal.

"Thank you Jesus,
For helping heal my wounds!"

Amen!

Story Behind the Poem

I don't remember the inspiration for this story. When I was writing my first book, *52 Pickup: These are the words I give to you to share with everyone*, I reviewed the manuscript over and over. When I came to this story, which was in the original *52 Pickup* manuscript, at one point, it didn't quite seem to fit. After a while, I replaced it with a different story called Perspective.

When I realized the theme of *Remember the Nails, 40 days of doing something uncomfortable on purpose*, this was one of the first stories that came to mind, because it would fit in perfectly.

Jesus was permanently wounded and suffered for us, because he loved us. Wounds ARE uncomfortable! I could finally see why this poem didn't fit before - it was supposed to go in this book instead. I love how that happened!   If you have a wound, I hope when you look at it, that you remember Jesus has wounds and he did it for you.

✝

Appendix

I hope you have found this book helpful in your attempt to think every day about doing Kingdom work. Being involved in ministry can sometimes be mundane, routine, or downright boring. There are many times where there is no glory or recognition. Much of the time it's like picking up trash: people will expect it to be done, and complain when it is not. You have to remind yourself that our Heavenly Father is watching our every move. It'll bring delight to him if your efforts are in his name, no matter the task, chore, or event.

There will be times others recognize your Kingdom work, so make sure when performing work in God's name, you are not looking for recognition from others. It has to be about the greater good and for the Kingdom of God. For example, my writing these poems and sharing them is something I struggle with. I don't know how people will use them, or how it'll impact their lives. I don't do it to hear the words, "Steve, you are a great author." From my perspective, every single thing in this book is God showing his grace and mercy, along with forgiving me for every wrong step I take, and every sin I commit. My goal is to be obedient, nothing more.

As of this writing, God has me on another journey to write a third book. The working title is *One Reason: 21 days to a New Beginning*. I figured after going through forty days of doing something uncomfortable on purpose, a fresh start and something less challenging would be welcomed. I do want to ask the question one last time, *"What on Earth are you doing for Heaven sakes?"* If your answer is something to forward the Kingdom of God, you are earning treasures in Heaven. The temporary discomfort here will be rewarded with an eternity of peace, joy and happiness.

God bless,

Steve Schofield

Credits and References

Not a Fan: Becoming a Completely Committed Follower of Jesus by Kyle Idleman (Author)
ISBN-10: 0310331935 or ISBN-13: 978-0310331933

http://www.southeastchristian.org/?page=3443

Mentioned in **What's in a Name section** - *Becoming a Contagious Christian* by Bill Hybels (Author) and Mark Mittelberg (Author)
ISBN-10: 0310210089 or ISBN-13: 978-0310210085

Day 10 – Everyday Porneia - *Real Marriage: The Trust About Sex, Friendship and Life Together* - Mark and Grace Driscoll (Authors)
ISBN-10: 1400205387 or ISBN-13: 978-1400205387

(More information on the word Porneia)
http://www.biblestudytools.com/lexicons/greek/nas/porneia.html

Day 12 - *Heaven Is for Real: A Little Boy's Astounding Story of His Trip to Heaven and Back* by Todd Burpo (Author) and Lynn Vincent (Author)
ISBN-10: 0849946158 or ISBN-13: 978-0849946158

Day 12 - *23 Minutes in Hell: One Man's Story About What He Saw, Heard, and Felt in that Place of Torment* by Bill Wiese (Author)
ISBN-10: 1591858828 or ISBN-13: 978-1591858829

Day 21—Live and Let Live – Tim Tebow: *Through My Eyes*
ISBN-10: 0062007289 or ISBN-13: 978-0062007285

Day 22 – Peaceful Servant - The Shack is located in Jugville, Michigan, USA: http://www.theshackbedandbreakfast.com/

Day 30 – Sharp - Comment used from James Watkins (www.jameswatkins.com): Author, Speaker

Day 32 – Thief - D.L. Moody on *Men of the Bible*
ISBN-10: 1935785826 or ISBN-13: 978-1935785828

Day 33 – Towards Home – *The Road Home* by Denise Jackson
ISBN-10: 140410531X or ASIN: B00IO9CE3W

About the Author

Steve Schofield was saved in 2005, and began writing poems shortly after that to deal with life's stresses. He lives in west Michigan with his wife Cindy and their three sons. They are active members of the Greenville Community Church. Steve is an IT professional, and has long been a self-described "internet geek," so he used that skill to develop a couple of successful online applications that fund his writing habit.

"I give thanks to God for using me to share these poems and stories. He has inspired me to tell them, and there were many times I could sense the Holy Spirit assisting me in my writing. There certainly is nothing like having our Creator speak directly to you; words can't describe it! I only hope that I can help someone else along their own path, whether they are Christian yet or not. I feel this is my purpose, and if I only reach one person... that would be enough."

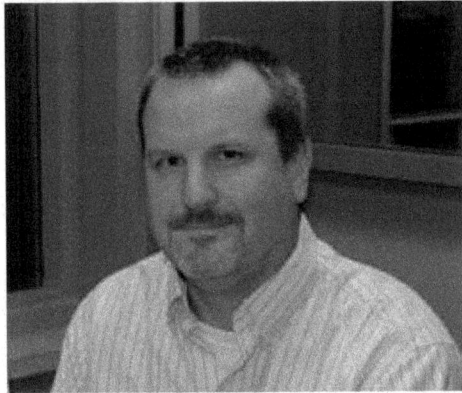

He is hard at work on his third book, which is also a devotional.

The author is also available for speaking engagements and other events. Visit his website, http://www.52pickup.co, for more information.

†